SEAFARERS OF THE
EMIRATES

AN ARABIAN ALBUM

SEAFARERS OF THE EMIRATES

AN ARABIAN ALBUM

A collection of mid-20th century photographs

RONALD CODRAI

MOTIVATE
PUBLISHING

Published with the encouragement and support of the
National Bank of Dubai

Dubai: PO Box 2331, Dubai, UAE
Tel: (+971 4) 282 4060, fax: (+971 4) 282 0428
e-mail: books@motivate.co.ae
www.booksarabia.com

Abu Dhabi: PO Box 43072, Abu Dhabi, UAE
Tel: (+971 2) 627 1666, fax: (+971 2) 627 1566

London: 4 Middle Street, London EC1A 7NQ
e-mail: motivateuk@motivate.co.ae

Directors:
Obaid Humaid Al Tayer and Ian Fairservice

Editorial team:
Justin Codrai and Ian Fairservice;
Alison Ashbee, Jackie Nel, Zelda Pinto and David Steele

Design:
Johnson Machado

ISBN 1 86063 132 0

British Library Cataloguing-in-Publication Data. A catalogue record
for this book is available from the British Library.

Printed by: Emirates Printing Press, Dubai

Foreword

Sitting in my office on the banks of Dubai Creek, in a modern building that reflects the unique maritime heritage of Dubai, it is my great pleasure to write this introduction to Ronald Codrai's new book, *Seafarers of the Emirates*.

Dubai owes its very existence to its location on the Arabian Gulf, and its history is closely intertwined with that of the mariners and traders who developed the various Sheikhdoms into the UAE. Sultan Ali Al-Owais, one of the founders of the National Bank of Dubai and its first Chairman, for example, was not only a pearl merchant but also the son of a pearl merchant. As you will read elsewhere in this book, he donated his priceless collection of pearls to the people of the UAE, under the custodianship of the National Bank of Dubai, thereby creating another link between the bank and the sea.

This collection is now housed in a dedicated museum in the National Bank of Dubai building, from where there are magnificent views of the Creek, the dhows moored below and the sea in the distance. It is entirely appropriate, then, that the bank should encourage and support the publication of this work. But there are other reasons too. . .

It was His Highness Sheikh Zayed bin Sultan Al Nahyan, President of the United Arab Emirates, Member of the Supreme Council and Ruler of Abu Dhabi, who said: "A people who do not know their past can have no present and no future," and it is the duty of companies such as the National Bank of Dubai to do everything in their power to help record and preserve our history and heritage for future generations.

Just before the discovery of oil and gas introduced sweeping changes, Ronald Codrai recorded the history of the Sheikhdoms – or Trucial States as they were known then (and even this name has a maritime connection). Now, some 50 years later, helping to preserve and showcase his work is – because of its maritime connections, historical value and artistic quality – so rewarding for us.

Codrai's photographs of the people and places of the Sheikhdoms provide a unique picture of life here during the middle of the last century. His photography is superb and would be the envy of many of today's professional photographers working with far more sophisticated equipment. Now we can see and enjoy another side of his work . . . his images of the skilled seafarers of this region, and the beautifully-crafted vessels they sailed.

Codrai's knowledge of Arabic must have been of enormous assistance in his work and he carefully noted everything he was photographing. So, many years later, he was able to write about what he had observed. As this book clearly illustrates, he had a deep affection for the places and people he studied and his eloquent work is noteworthy for its accuracy, compassion and humour.

These are the ingredients for a great new work. It is a tribute to the brave mariners who for hundreds of years sailed from the Gulf to distant ports and the hardy men who harvested the riches of the sea, whether fishermen or pearl divers. I know it will be treasured by all those who have a fondness for the sea and a love of Arabia.

Abdullah Mohamed Saleh
Managing Director of the National Bank of Dubai

Other Motivate titles by Ronald Codrai

Dubai – An Arabian Album
Abu Dhabi – An Arabian Album
Sharjah and the North-East Sheikhdoms – An Arabian Album
Travels to Oman – An Arabian Album
One Second in the Arab World
Faces of the Emirates

COVER: A *kutiyah* under full sail, homeward bound to Dubai from Africa, and carrying a full cargo of mangrove poles (*chandals*), spices and cloth.

HALF-TITLE PAGE: A *boom* at anchorage at Khorfakkan, the last safe anchorage between the Gulf and Muscat.

TITLE SPREAD: A *jelbut* with sails trimmed but still at anchor – and waiting for the tide in Dubai Creek. Only a small number of *jelbuts* were fitted with engines then.

PREVIOUS SPREAD: This photograph was taken on the curve of the Creek at which Sindagha was separated from Dubai. In the foreground, a *jelbut* has been hauled ashore and is undergoing repairs – a *barasti* (*'arish*), or palm-frond shelter – has been constructed over its poop deck.

Dedication

To Pamela

Ronald and Pamela Codrai on honeymoon in 1952.

I dedicate this book to my beloved and brave wife who, during our many years of marriage, has always been supportive of me in whatever I have been engaged or wherever I have been posted. Sometimes this was in dangerous or adverse circumstances and, throughout our life together, she has quietly and bravely borne the cross of her disability from the polio she contracted while we were on our honeymoon. Even so, she gave birth to, and admirably raised, our two sons, Christian and Justin.

I had intended to present her with this book as my present to her on our Golden Wedding Anniversary on February 26, 2002 – as it contains some golden memories of our life on the Trucial Coast during our marriage.

Unfortunately, just before the millennium, while working on other books, I was informed that I was terminally ill with only a very short time to live. I accept this as a challenge and, *insha'allah* (a phrase I have used many times but never so meaningfully as now), I will fulfil my intention. If, however, my time runs out before our anniversary, I earnestly hope my sons will complete and, with Ian Fairservice's help, publish this book and present it to their mother in the year of the 50th anniversary of our blessed wedding, with all my love and gratitude.

Ronald Codrai
January 12, 2000

Contents

A returning pearling vessel, eagerly rowed into port by its fit crew at the end of the pearl harvest.

Introduction

*"And among His signs are the ships,
like mountains on the sea:*

*If He will He calmeth the winds so that
they become motionless . . .*

Or He causeth them to perish. . . ."

Al Koran, **Sura V (97)**

In an anomaly of geography, the Trucial States bordering the Arabian Gulf derived much of their character from their desert territories, but the sea that lapped their shores contributed most towards their survival and economic viability. This was particularly so where those coastlines had natural harbours and sheltered anchorages. Backed by a difficult terrain of mountains and desert, the Trucial States depended heavily on the sea for their communications and for importing many of their basic requirements. The sea yielded an abundance of seafood, provided a means of trade and contained rich oyster beds yielding some of the finest pearls that gave rise to a trade which, by contrast with the barest level of subsistence that was then the norm, provided a period of relative prosperity.

At one time or another, the lives of a large proportion of the people of the Trucial States – the name given to the United Arab Emirates before 1971 – were orientated towards the sea. In summer, they converged on the small seaports to join the pearling boats and, if they lived on the coast, they would probably have been engaged in fishing activities; these were the seasonal seafarers. Although some Bedu might never have seen the sea and some seafarers had never travelled into the desert, it was not uncommon for the activities of the seafarers and desert folk to overlap to the point where the same people who shinned up palm trees to harvest dates would shin up the masts of ocean-going vessels to haul up the sails. Those whose livelihoods were wholly dependent on the sea were the regular mariners; the men who manned the trading vessels that plied the seas to places near and far. They sailed the traditional craft on long voyages to India, Southern Arabia and East Africa as well as to other parts of the Gulf.

From Bestrew in the northernmost corner of the Gulf, down through the narrow straits in the south where the Arabian Gulf joins the Gulf of Oman which runs out into the vast Indian Ocean, the lateen sail would be sighted everywhere, a symbol of the same age-old marine tradition. From pearl diving to fishing to country-craft trading between ports and villages in the Gulf or on lengthy voyages to India and Africa, all were engaged in eking out a living from the sea.

The purpose of this book is to place on record the last years of the old way of life on the Trucial Coast as it related to the sea; a time when the Gulf could claim to have been the home of the largest surviving merchant sailing fleet in the world. I lived in Dubai in the middle of the 20th century and was privileged to have been able to see, record, experience and photograph much of that marine activity at a time when the Trucial Coast was on the threshold of radical change – change that later led to the virtual demise of marine activity with the waning of the last days of the distinctive lateen sails and change that led to a new form of trade – the oil trade.

As I left Dubai in 1955, the owners of the vessels (particularly the *jelbuts*) were doing their best to adapt them to the work of the modern era, not least of which was in connection with the seismic operations of the oil companies. On more

than one occasion, in the shallow, reef-laden seas of the Arabian Gulf, they proved their advantage over other types of craft. However, the cost of new vessels had risen sharply, as had the cost of labour. Even then, the cost of keeping a crew at sea on a long sailing voyage was a not-inconsiderable item of expenditure. The pearling industry was already in severe decline and the pearling vessels then in service were only a fraction of their former number. However, the freight rates of the larger vessels still compared favourably with those of the steamers and there was work to be had.

During the course of the years, some material in this book has been published in features and in some of my other books. I have attempted here to gather it together with other unused material to provide a more complete picture of this all-but-forgotten period in the history of the Gulf. It is my hope that this book will go some way towards

conjuring up in the reader's mind the proud seafaring traditions, boat-building and maritime trading of the Trucial States of old which have contributed so much to the highly distinctive character of the present-day United Arab Emirates.

Editors' note: The term 'Trucial States' is the former name of the seven Arab sheikhdoms on the Arabian Gulf which were to become the United Arab Emirates (UAE) and refers to the 1836 Maritime Truce between Britain and these sheikhdoms. It was only after their independence in 1971 that the Trucial States became known as the Emirates; this book refers accordingly.

A pearling boat arrives in Dubai Creek: For the homecoming crew, the joy of returning to their families was heightened or tempered by the success of the season's harvest.

Chapter one

Historical background

As far back as pre-Islamic times, ports such as Bahrain, Muscat and Sur were important centres of trade and navigation, for the waters of the Arabian Gulf were sailed by the early Assyrians of Iraq and, possibly, even by their predecessors. There is interesting historical evidence (including a clay tablet discovered at Ur which lists merchandise imported from these places) to show that sea voyages along the coast of the Arabian Peninsula were not uncommon in the first half of the Third Millennium.

One theory names the Phoenicians as being the skilled navigators responsible for this trade, but that is largely a matter of conjecture. More certain is that the Arabian Gulf was the scene of later Babylonian sea power as the Neo-Babylonians were a people no less proud of their ships than of their cities and ramparts.

After the Babylonian era, interest in the navigation of the Arabian Gulf seemed to suffer a decline and it was not until the conquests of Alexander that the exploration of these waters received a new impetus. It was under his orders (in 326 BC) that Admiral Nearchus made his famous voyage in the Arabian Gulf though, like so many of the early voyages of exploration, it was mainly confined to the Persian, rather than the Arabian, side of the Gulf.

Much has yet to be discovered and unravelled before the early history of navigation in the Arabian Gulf is at all complete, as references to the subject are widely scattered and mainly very brief. However, the mere existence of the flimsiest

The stark, rugged outline of Ras Haffah, in Ra's al-Khaimah, just north of Dibba, as seen from the air.

references makes positive the antiquity of seafaring there. Someday, perhaps in a desert far from the sea, a spade may uncover an archaeological discovery that will shed new light on the story. Until then, the early history of these waters must remain largely hypothetical.

It was not until the first years of Islam that the veil over our knowledge of the Gulf began to lift, as it was with the coming of Islam (and, for a time, the establishment of its political centre in Iraq) that the spirit of enterprise and exploration in the Gulf received its impetus. By the 10th century, ships from the Gulf had reached Canton, which became an emporium for trade with China. Muslim sailors and traders reached far-flung places such as Sind, Korea, Japan, Ceylon, Madagascar and the East coast of Africa. (Some confusion exists in the early chronicles of Arab travel in that the Arabic name for Madagascar, *Waqwaq,* is the same as for Japan. In the Levant, the 'Islands of *Waqwaq*' is still used in colloquial Arabic as an expression for a mythical or far-away place, without necessarily meaning either Japan or Madagascar.)

Being linked to Baghdad by the big waterways of Iraq, the Arabian Gulf route soon became an instrument of world trade, particularly during Abassid times. In this way, Baghdad obtained the silks, frankincense, spices, ivory, wood, nuts and other luxuries of the East (as no doubt it had done in Assyrian and Babylonian times, albeit on a smaller scale).

These wares then found their way across the ancient caravan routes of the Islamic countries to Europe which, at that time, had no direct link with the East. As a result, the pre-Islamic caravan routes flourished during Islamic times but never reached the same importance as the routes to India and China as these places became more easily accessible by sea.

The long history of navigation centred in the Arabian Gulf, and the great seafaring tradition that was borne of it, prepared the way for mariners of other nations who later sailed the Indian Ocean and the Arabian Gulf. It was an Arab Pilot, Ahmed bin Majid, who is chronicled as having shown Vasco da Gama the way to India after the latter's circumnavigation of Africa in 1498. Ahmed bin Majid was already known as the author of the *Arab*

A typical waterfront scene at Khorfakkan, Kalba, photographed in 1949 – note the fortress stategically situated on the beach.

Sailing Manuals of the Arabian Gulf and Indian Ocean of that time, and some Arab historians attribute the invention of the compass to him, although the claim is not entirely substantiated.

Having glanced briefly at some of the background, and taking into account the considerable prowess and exploration successes of the Arab seafarers of the Arabian Gulf, and their substantial knowledge of the Indian Ocean, you might wonder why they penetrated as far as India, China and Africa but did not develop the route to the Isthmus of Suez and, from there, to the Mediterranean. The seafaring tradition of the Arabs and Phoenicians of the Mediterranean, and of the Arabs of the Gulf and Indian Ocean, have little in common with each other. The probable reason for this was twofold; the first being a lack of incentive. The overland trading routes were well established, particularly after the rise of Islam, and this caused the merchant adventurers to concentrate on the south and east in search of greater rewards than they could expect from hazardous and feared journeys through the Red Sea – the very entrance to this sea was known as the *Bab al Mandab* (The Strait of Tears).

The second reason was what might be described as political considerations. With Christian shipping plying the Mediterranean, and with the piercing of the Isthmus of Suez (an idea ascribed to some of the early Abassid Caliphs), it was always considered a great danger to the strategic safety of the Islamic World and, what is more, to the heart of Islam itself – the Holy Cities of the Hedjaz. Moreover, to each other, Christian and Muslim sailors were nothing but brigands.

Whatever the reasons, both historically and contemporarily, Arab navigation in Eastern waters remained isolated from the Mediterranean, to follow the same traditions that survived until recent times.

Interestingly, the nautical vocabulary of the Arabian Gulf has absorbed many English terms such as *Djeeb*, meaning jib sail; *Manawar*, meaning man-of-war or warships in general; *Boy*, meaning buoy; *F'stma'l*, meaning fast mail on the BI Steamers and *Meyana*, meaning main mast. In addition, 'stop', 'slow', 'fast' and others were in current use and had been assimilated since the introduction of marine engines.

There are, of course, also many Arabic words that have been similarly assimilated into English, such as 'Admiral' (from *Emir al Bahr*), 'cable',

Above: An aerial view of Dubai, taken in 1951. You can see the three districts of Dubai's Creek – Dubai proper to the right, Deira across the Creek and Shindagha trailing across the sea. **Top:** A view of Abu Dhabi in 1949 – the Ruler's fort, Qasr Al Hosn, is clearly visible on the outskirts of the main settlement. **Right:** Dubai Creek, with Sharjah in the distant background.

'average', 'sloop', 'barque' and 'monsoon'.

It may also be of interest to note that 'Trafalgar' is from the Arabic *Al Taraf al Aghar* (Cape of the Cave) and there is also the amusing suggestion that 'Britannic' comes from the Arabic *Barr al Tannakeh* (Coast of Tinsmiths).

The sea was a great provider for the people of the Trucial States. As well as affording them their easiest means of communication, it yielded the oysters which gave them their famous pearling industry, produced coral stone for building and provided them with a great variety of edible fish. Although the Ancient Greeks never actively visited this coastline of southeastern Arabia, they called it the 'Coast of Fish-eaters' (*Ichthyophagi*). This was probably gleaned from hearsay by Admiral Nearchus on his travels and was not an inapt description which would probably have applied equally to most parts of the Gulf. In any event, it is probably the existence of such bountiful sea life that gave rise to the early habitation of the Trucial Coast and from which, naturally, the boat-building stemmed that eventually led to the trading and seafaring traditions that are so much a part of the Emirates today.

Barasti (palm-frond) dwellings grouped together on the Creek side of Dubai, with Shindagha in the background. *Barastis* were unfortunately often damaged or even destroyed by storms.

Chapter two

Sea of abundance

"The game of the sea is lawful for you. . . ."

Al Koran, Sura V (97)

Without doubt, the people of the Trucial States were very fortunate in having such splendid food, that formed an important part of their diet, so easily available. On or near the shores where it was caught or landed, it was eaten fresh or sun-dried by the people of the hinterland and the mountains.

Totalling some 540 kilometres in length, the coastline was split into two by the protrusion of the tip of the Hajar range of mountains which formed part of the territory of the Sultanate of Oman. Each of the divided stretches of coastline was distinct in character, while the two seas of the Trucial States had several natural differences.

On the east coast, the Gulf of Oman was enriched by a strong upsurge from the Indian Ocean, where its abundant growth of plankton ensured its waters were kept well stocked with a rich supply of many types of fish which were easily netted close to the shore.

This made it possible for the people settled on this eastern coast to mix their fishing activities with their work in the palm groves or on other forms of agriculture.

Flowing through the Straits of Hormuz, the Gulf of Oman also served to enrich the waters of the southern part of the Arabian Gulf, as well as

Sardine fishing was an important part of the daily chores and formed a necessary element of the staple diet.

stocking it with fish such as mackerel, barracuda and sardines, from its less saline waters. Every year, hundreds of sailing craft from the Arabian Gulf would pass through the Gulf of Oman, as would vessels from Oman itself, on long trading voyages to India and Africa. It was their gateway to the world.

When calm, the shallower waters of the southern Arabian Gulf was a sea of many different hues – various shades of green, blue and turquoise – which would vary with the depth of water and the state of the sky. A light breeze would create twinkling ripples along the shore and around any small protrusions of rock or sand, while the strong, hot, southerly wind would cause a waveless swell which seemed to be trying to push the sea back to where it originated. Not so the infamous northwesterly, the *shamal*, which made the sea a foaming mass along the Trucial States' windward shore, closing the entrances to its creeks and treating the sailing craft with a great contempt that

LEFT AND ABOVE: After much chanting, the catch was carried ashore and scattered over the sand to dry in the sun.

tested them and the seafaring skills of their crews to the limits.

Thought to be one of the newest seas on this planet, the Arabian Gulf is also said to be one of its richest fishing areas, its stretches of underwater meadows providing ample food and good breeding conditions for a massive marine population which has successfully adapted to the Gulf's salty waters (nearly twice as salty as the oceans because of its shallowness and high rate of evaporation).

While I was not very knowledgeable as to the different types of fish in the Gulf, it was quite obvious from those which I caught, saw on sale in the souk or had the considerable pleasure of tasting, that they were of immense variety. Not knowing their English names, I learned and noted the names of some in Arabic. Among them were the *Chanad, Hamour* (the grouper or rock-cod of the Gulf), *Balool, Biyah, Rabeel, Safi, Shaary* and *Sikin*, as well as sharks, barracuda, sawfish, stingrays, bonefish and, of course, shellfish, including the famous oyster.

The Gulf was also a good breeding ground for shrimp, though the only time I saw them was when sold in the souk, sun-dried and salted. In that state, they looked far from appetising and, on seeing them, a Bedu once commented to me that he preferred the 'flying shrimps' (locusts). Then there were the sea turtles which returned, year after year, to the same breeding grounds on the sandy beaches where their ping-pong-sized, pliable eggs were sometimes collected and eaten, being 'good for the back', an imaginative association no doubt with the turtle's shell.

A strange and less common product from the sea was ambergris, a dark, tar-like substance sometimes found floating in the Gulf. Used as a base in the making of perfume, it was a valuable find. Moreover, it was evidence of the presence of whales, one of which I saw spouting in the sea on the northern side of Cape Musandam during spring.

It was not until my first journey on a local craft, a *jelbut*, that I became fully aware of the extent to which the waters of the Gulf were such prolific providers. I had left it to the *Nakhuda* (plural *Nawakhid*, a shipmaster or captain – one of the many Persian words found in the nautical vocabulary of the Gulf Arabs) to obtain provisions and it was not until we were at sea that I enquired as to the ship's fare. This caused some amusement among the crew who cried out, "Everything, everything!". In fact, we had rice, ghee, flour, onions,

TOP AND BOTTOM LEFT: Fishermen were seldom people with a single vocation, alternating between other work according to the seasons and whatever opportunities lay at sea or on shore, such as tending the date groves. Some were also Bedu, and would head off into the desert to tend their camels.

TOP, ABOVE AND OVERLEAF: When a school of sardines was sighted, the boat would circle it back to shore where all hands waited to haul in the catch.

green limes, tea, coffee, sugar and, of course, a large wooden tank of sweet water. Everything?

As soon as we had cleared the shallows, a trolling-spoon was let out on a line on either side of the stern and, from then on, we hauled in a marvellous and varied supply of fish. Gently cooked and served on a bed of rice with chopped, raw onions and a good squeeze of lime, the fish was superb. Of all the fish I have eaten in my life, I still remember it as being among the best and I never tired of the same fare for every meal other than breakfast, when we had a toasted mixture of flour, sugar and water with our tea and coffee. I was soon looking forward to lunch and it was not long before our sea-lines had hooked it.

The subject of bait gave rise to a lengthy discussion and some ribald jokes but, on this occasion, we were using silver trolling-spoons which the *Nakhuda* had bought on a visit to Bahrain. For sure they were very good, though the sceptical crew would not acknowledge them as being as good as their own choices of bait. "Hold up a lime," said one of them, a sailor originally from Socotra, "and a fish will soon join it." Frequently, the lines had to be pulled in because our needs had already been met.

On another trip, with a borrowed rod, I caught what the crew acclaimed to be the mother-and-father of all barracudas. It was very old. Close up, I was able to see its frightful interlocking, backwards-sloping teeth and I understood why some feared it more than the shark. Insisting it was some kind of a record, the *Nakhuda* took a photograph of me holding the fish and the crew kept its head, the stink of which steadily increased until we reached journey's end. My camera smelled of it for some time and later, after landing, my host was not appreciative when it was placed on my rucksack in one of his bedrooms!

Apart from this trolling of lines from sea-going vessels, several traditional methods of fishing were employed in the Trucial States, mostly from or near to the shores. Whether full-time or seasonal fishermen, all were closely acquainted with the main movement of the fish which, in general, was into the warmer, shallow waters in winter and to the cooler, deeper waters in summer. The fishermen were also well acquainted with the different areas of underwater weeds to which the fish were attracted in the shallower waters.

During the winter, most of the people living in the palm-frond huts along the shore would be

THIS SPREAD: After the sardines had dried in the sun, the women and children would pick out any larger fish. The rest of the sardines were gathered and used as cattle food or fertiliser – one of Dubai's few exports at the time.

engaged in catching sprats for which there was a good demand for use as animal fodder and fertiliser, both in the Trucial States and abroad. In fact, of the estimated 8,000 to 12,000 tons caught annually, more than half was shipped abroad – a small but most welcome export trade which helped to pay for some of the basic foodstuffs, such as rice and flour, which had to be imported.

Men in a small boat would take out a long drift-net (similar to a seine-net in England) a short distance from the shore and, when a shoal of sprats was in position between the boat and the shore, the net would be dropped and its ends taken round the shoal to the shore where other men would slowly haul them in, the two groups of haulers moving closer to each other in the process. The nets were usually about 100 feet long and, as they were drawn in, the excitement of the people on shore increased. Leaping fish agitated the water as they were pulled into an ever-decreasing space, while the boatmen banged the sides of their boat and the haulers chanted louder and louder as their families moved down to where the catch would be landed. It was only when the last of the net was being

RIGHT: A young boy cleaning his rather good catch – the Gulf waters abounded with fish.
ABOVE: A stingray caught off the coast of Dubai – as many as a dozen stingrays could be caught in one large net.

dragged in that the size of the catch could be seen.

Women moved in to take any larger, palatable fish to their huts, while children joined their fathers in emptying the net, then spreading the large mound of wriggling sprats about the beach to dry in the sun. In one net, I saw around a dozen stingrays, an unpleasant reminder of their presence in the shallow waters. In other nets were several small sharks. Gathering the spread-out mass of sprats after they had dried was a tedious task, as many became trodden into the sand. They were then loaded on camels or donkeys and taken to the palm groves or wherever there was a market for them, perhaps across the sands at the inland settlements. Others would be loaded into a boat and carried to the nearest coastal town where they were being amassed until there was a sufficient quantity for a shipment abroad. All this activity entailed much hard work but, on the whole, spratting time was a happy period along the coast.

Another method of fishing was the use of the *gargour*, a hemispherical trap of up to six to eight feet in diameter made of either wire mesh or closely-latticed palm fronds. With bait placed inside, it would be lowered into the sea from a fishing boat and its line attached to a marker float. It was very effective, and would be pulled up to empty its catch every day or so.

I was surprised not to have seen the highly successful *hadra* type of fish trap of Bahrain in greater use. It was made of palm fronds closely staked into the seabed in shallow waters in a 'V' or curved shape in which fish would be left after the tide had receded. The lack of use was possibly because the Gulf Coast of the Trucial States was a windward shore, since I did once see what appeared to be the remains of a *hadra* type of trap on the leeside of one of the islands off the coast of Abu Dhabi.

On two occasions I saw, along the isolated, westernmost shores of Abu Dhabi, the remains of what appeared to be a sea cow. This remarkable mammal, of more than six feet in length, suckles its young on milk, breathes air and has short hairs on

LEFT: Carrying the day's catch from the beach. Note the drying sardines in the background.

Overleaf: Leaving more sardines out to dry – the bigger fish, kept for human consumption, were extremely rich in vitamin E and other valuable nutrients.

its body. Being herbivorous, this dugong, to give its correct name, must have enjoyed the nearby underwater meadows which may well have enticed it into the shallow waters in which it became grounded and then washed ashore. I asked local fishermen about it and found that it was also called sea cow in Arabic (*Baqarat al Bahr*). They said it was caught and eaten very infrequently. Apart from this I was able to glean little, except that one man thought it was related to the whale, which he personally had only sighted once in his life.

A colourful variety of shells could be found along the shores of the Trucial States, and my wife and I collected a large number which we later donated to a museum in America. It identified many as somewhat rare and unexpected finds in the Gulf region. Our collecting activities amused our younger friends, who were curious and puzzled to know what new or strange use we had found for the shells, perhaps trying to associate them with the precious finds from the oyster and the minor export trade in oyster shells. The outcome was that children would appear wherever

we went, producing shells which they had kept for us and, sometimes, we would find little heaps of shells on our doorstep.

At night, whether aboard a vessel or crossing a creek in an *abra*, the slightest agitation of the sea would produce a beautiful show of fluorescence. It varied greatly according to light from the sky and the state of the sea but, at times, it dripped from the oars like pearls being trickled back into the sea. The darkness of night might also be broken by the illuminated shape of a sea snake wriggling past. Sailors said that only its underside was 'lit up', so it swam on its back at night, near to the surface, so as not to be seen by large fish in the depths.

RIGHT: A fishing boat is hauled ashore after a hard day's work.
ABOVE: At some time or another, but usually in summer, the Shihuh tribesmen descended from their mountain homes to the sandy coves and strips of shoreline to catch their fish.

PREVIOUS SPREAD: Fishing nets were valuable possessions and were made – and repaired – by hand.

Possibly, but what creature would want to attack and eat this venomous creature, its poison being some 10 times stronger than that of the cobra?

It was not until many years after I had left the Gulf that I read of an expert estimate of there being 200 different species of fish there, including many with somewhat bizarre names in English such as the Painted Grunt, the Starry Blowfish, the White-spotted Guitar Fish, the Bearded Mud Skipper, the Penant Butterflyfish and the Arabian Barred Killifish! Had I known with whom I was sharing the water, and not forgetting the sharks, stingrays, sea snakes and barracudas, as well as the Portuguese men-of-war, it might have spoiled some of the considerable pleasure I had from my daily dips in the bountiful waters off the Trucial Coast.

LEFT: Carrying a *gargour*, or fish trap. The *gargour*, made of wire or latticed palm fronds, was usually emptied every few days.
ABOVE: Bait was placed inside the *gargour*, then it was lowered into the sea from a boat and a line was attached to a float.

OVERLEAF: A swarm of locusts over Dubai Creek in 1953.

ABOVE: Fishermen untangle their nets at Khorfakkan – while a distinctive high-sterned *baggarah*, used mainly in the waters of the Gulf of Oman, waits in the background.

LEFT: Locusts were known as 'flying shrimps' – people would collect them in hurriedly-shed *ghutras* (headcloths) or *wazars* (loincloths), then feed them to their camels or donkeys, sell them in the souks . . . or simply munch on them.

ABOVE: A seasoned fisherman from the Jumeirah area casts an appraising eye over the waters.
LEFT: Fishermen going about their daily work – but come the next season, they might well be diving for pearls or tending date-palm groves.

**ABOVE: A lone fisherman sets off in a small *shasha*. The author
only saw these simple but ingeniouly made craft on the coast
of the Gulf of Oman, in places where the palm tree abounded.**

ABOVE: A Gulf fisherman shows off his catch – a superb Kingfish. This photograph was taken off Ras al Jibal in 1948.

OVERLEAF: At low tide, only craft of the shallowest draught, such as this small fishing boat, could navigate the entrance to Dubai Creek (known as 'The Bar').

LEFT: Vessels at anchor in Sharjah Creek – most that entered the Creek were of the shallower draught *jelbut* or *sambuq* type, as the larger *booms* could barely enter when fully laden and, as a result, their cargoes had first to be ferried ashore.

ABOVE: Khorfakkan's natural harbour sheltered countless seafarers in stormy weather, while the small town was always a good source of fresh supplies.

PREVIOUS SPREAD: A fishing boat off Ra's al-Khaimah – the barren Hajar Mountains yielded little to sustain the few people who lived there, so the nutritious fish from the surrounding seas were indeed a blessing.

Above: Supper – a barracuda caught off the coast of Dubai.
Top: Selling fish in the souk, where women often sold the catch obtained by their husbands.
Left: Carrying the catch to market, in Sharjah.

Previous spread: At the fish market – not surprisingly, the coastal people were fastidious selectors of their fish from the souk and this fish market, which developed on a small open space where the catches were landed. Most of the small stalls were covered with palm fronds for protection from the sun.

61

Chapter three

Pearl-diving

Every summer, the waterfronts of the ports scattered along the shores of the Trucial Coast would hum with activity as chanting crews prepared their boats for the annual pearling season. "After tea drink the waters of bitterness," (myrrh water, which is used as a medicine), they sang as they hauled into the water the small wooden craft on which they would endure several months of hardship and privation.

The same scene had been re-enacted for countless years but, in the late 1940s, comparatively few boats departed for the pearling banks. Few, that is, compared with earlier in the century when upwards of 4,000 boats manned by tens of thousands of men were engaged in harvesting the pearls in the Gulf. The decline started at the beginning of the 1930s when the Japanese developed and started marketing the 'cultured' pearl. At about the same time, the main markets in the West for the Gulf's pearls were hit by both recession and a change in fashion, followed by World War Two. The Gulf's trade in pearls never recovered from these events and its final demise came with the arrival of the oil era.

In the late 1940s and early 1950s, 'the dive' was still a main feature of life on the Trucial Coast and, although only a small proportion of those with experience in the industry were still employed, there were many optimists who believed there would be a revival and a return to the prosperity of earlier years.

The famous pearl banks of the Gulf lay, more or less, in an area bounded by the coast of Eastern and Southeastern Arabia and a line drawn from Kuwait in the north, to Sharjah in the south. The formation of the seabed, the temperature and shallowness of

A pearl merchant, or *tawash*, weighing pearls on a brass scale, using polished marble weights and a compendium of sizes, weights and grades.

those waters were, apparently, all favourable to the growth of the pearl-bearing oyster. The pearling banks there had been fished since the earliest times and yielded some of the finest pearls in the world. The majority of boats from the Trucial Coast operated in the waters between Abu Dhabi and Qatar where there were innumerable pearling banks and many small islands to which the boats could run for shelter and supplies.

Although some diving took place in the spring and autumn, the principal pearling season started around the middle of May and, with the exception of Ramadan, when all the boats returned to harbour, lasted about four months. During winter, the sea was too cold and the winds too uncertain for pearl-diving but, in the heat of summer, the sea was warm and usually calm and the divers were able to operate without the added discomfort of the cold. Indeed, the summers could be so intense that, after a strenuous day of diving, the crew would continually seek relief from the heat by slipping over the sides of the crowded boats into the green waters.

The method of harvesting was extremely simple and remained the same through the ages. On arriving at the banks, the diver descended by putting his foot on a small stone attached to a rope played out by a hauler. His only other aid was a wooden or bone clip, like the old type of clothes-peg, which he slid over his nostrils. Sometimes, if he was working on a bank where the oysters were attached to coral, he protected his fingers by wearing leather fingerstalls or, if the sea was infested with jellyfish, he protected his body and head with a cotton garment.

Before descending, the diver did not take a deep breath, as might be supposed, but simply breathed very deeply for a minute or two before taking a last light breath followed by the plunge. As soon as he reached the bottom, he would immediately begin collecting the oysters which he would put into a small, net-type basket attached to the hauling line. When the basket was full, he would jerk on the line and the hauler would swiftly pull him up.

On rising to the surface, the diver would take a short rest while remaining in the water and holding on to a rope attached to an overhanging oar. Not all the divers were in the water at the same time, and they averaged about half-an-hour's diving

A pearling vessel being rowed into port at the end of a season – blessed relief for the divers on board.

each before resting in the boat. The usual total diving time for a day would be two to three hours, during which time a diver would probably descend between 70 to 100 times.

Diving operations usually took place in water from 25 to 50 feet deep, but some of the richest banks were much deeper and divers would sometimes have to descend to 100 feet. They were able to stay down only from a half to one-and-a-half minutes and only a few were able to stay down for this longer time – exceptional divers could stay down for nearly two minutes. The capability of a diver depended as much on his daring as on his constitution, and those who had earned the reputation of being unafraid to dive in deep waters were rated well above their normal market value.

A diver might be expected to bring up from three to 20 oysters at a time but, all too frequently, he would appear empty-handed. The luckiest haul at any time was a *Tabrah*, a cluster of oysters which were said to nearly always be pearl-bearing – on some occasions, they could represent the profits of an entire season.

Throughout the day's diving operations, the boat would be constantly changing position by being allowed to drift away from its dropped anchor, then being hauled back along the anchor-line by the crew. It was customary, when hauling the boat to a new position, for it to be done as rapidly as the agile bodies of the crew would permit. This was done to the chanting of one or two shrill voices matched against a chorus of deep grunts.

The pearling boats were all local types of wooden sailing craft with lateen rigs, ranging from the small *shahuf*, to the *jelbut*, *sambuq* and, sometimes, the *boom*. The centuries-old designs were, with the exception of the *boom*, highly suitable for operating in shallow waters.

Although casualties occurred every year, divers were not often molested by sharks, barracudas, swordfish or any of the other large fish found in the Arabian Gulf. However, they dreaded the stingray, which could inflict a painful sting that sometimes resulted in a fever lasting several days.

The crew of a large boat was composed of the captain, the divers, the haulers, a cook and one or two boys to cater for the simple needs of the others. Although many of the crew were attracted into employment by the prospects of a good share of the profits at the end of the season, most had little choice as to their employment.

The opening of oysters was usually done by the

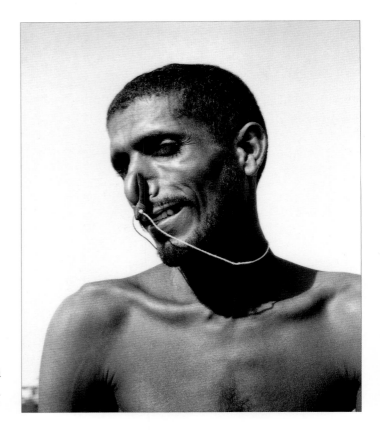

sick and the aged in the evening or early morning and was very closely watched by the captain and, on a large boat, by one or two invigilators. Every pearl found would be passed to the captain. Disciplinary action was taken against anyone caught trying to conceal a pearl, although such attempts were very rare. The actual task of opening the oysters was unpleasant because of the smell and the task was made even worse by the insects frequently attracted by it.

Young oysters were returned to the sea together with most of the shells, only the largest being kept for sale to a merchant dealing in mother-of-pearl. One of my neighbours in Dubai was such a merchant, and he would accumulate the shells until he had a sufficient quantity to ship to Germany, where they were used mainly for making buttons. I could never understand why greater use was not made of mother-of-pearl when a small sphere of the same substance was worth so much.

Occasionally, a pearl would be found embedded

RIGHT: Taking a break: A diver rests in the water between dives, clinging to one of the many ropes dangling from oars overhanging the pearling vessel.
ABOVE: A pearl diver wearing a nose clip made of bone.

ABOVE: A *saib,* **the hauler on whom a diver depended to swiftly pull him to the surface as soon as he tugged on the hauling rope. Here, he is holding a** *diyyin* **(basket), into which a diver would place his find of oysters.**

TOP: Pearls in the oyster shells in which they were found. There were wide variations in the size of both oyster and shell – and the size gave no clue as to whether or not they were pearl-bearing. These were two small sized oysters. Note the beautiful mixture of pearls in one of the shells.

RIGHT: A pearl diver wearing protective clothing – a one-piece cotton suit, worn when occasion demanded, to safeguard him from Portuguese men-of-war and jellyfish, with their ugly stings. These were encountered in large numbers in summer.

in the mother-of-pearl-covered shell and would be dug out or the shell might contain many tiny seed pearls – there were a great many variations in the finds and I found it exciting to watch the shells being opened. The tired crew, however, regarded it as just another chore, although the financial outcome of the season depended on the finds.

Ear trouble, of which there was plenty, particularly among newer divers, was dealt with by the 'hot-iron' treatment which was also used for most other ailments – the tip of a heated iron was applied to the affected part.

A severe flogging was the punishment for an inattentive hauler who had risked a diver's life. Sometimes, either because of the actions of the hauler or those of the diver, a diver in deep water would misjudge his underwater duration and fill up with water as he was being hauled to the surface. He would emerge only to sink again and be carried away by the tide.

Occasionally, a diver would suffer a temporary form of madness and, to dispossess him of the evil spirit, he would be covered with a sail while, often for long periods, a member of the crew read the Koran over him.

Nearly all the divers had, at one time or another, suffered underwater hallucinations – to the divers, practically every oddity that occurred to them was attributed to the *jinns* rather than to the effects of their underwater feats. There were very few divers who did not claim to have endured weird spectacles in the silent depths – headless camels, cutlass-wielding women and monsters with multiple heads were among the many frightening sights they said they had encountered.

Social life for the crews, during the long periods at sea, was confined to visiting nearby boats, exchanging news and, perhaps, drinking coffee with their friends. Conditions on board were nearly always cramped and, all too frequently, there was not enough space for stretching out and sleeping properly, particularly on the smaller boats.

During the day, the divers ate only a few dates, the main meal being at night which, while supplies lasted, usually consisted of something with rice. If supplies were short and they had been unable to catch any fish, the crew would occasionally eat the oyster meat (which was also sometimes dried, salted and taken off to the Buraimi group of oases where it was eaten by the Bedu when it was several months old). The supply of fresh water had to be used very sparingly on the pearling boats as, once it was

exhausted, the crew either had to return to port or purchase it from trading boats at a very high price.

Scientific accounts of the growth of pearls meant as little in the Arabian Gulf during my time there as they did in England at a time when pearls were believed to be 'angels' tears'. The pearlers of the Gulf believed that pearls were 'rain drops', and even the knowledge of how cultured pearls were created did not alter this belief – the pearling season following a wet winter was always thought to be a good one.

Towards the end of September, the boats began to return from the pearling banks. Chanting loudly in rhythm with the oars, the high-spirited crews rowed the last two or three miles into harbour, splashing, rather than pulling on, as many as 20 oars with three men on each oar – an impressive spectacle, as the crews intended it to be. It ended with a cheer as the anchor was dropped and the boat came to rest.

Rowing boats would bring alongside the pearl merchants and each little shape of soft lustre in the captain's purse would embark on the next stage of its long, adventurous journey – a journey that would take it from hand to hand through many countries, leaving some richer, and a few poorer, for its passing. Only a small number of pearls remained in the Trucial States as there were few who could afford the luxury of their splendour; also, fashion favoured gold, rather than pearls, as

an adornment for the womenfolk.

Financial arrangements for crew and boat were worked out according to a fixed system that seldom varied. At the start of the season, the merchant who owned the boat would buy food for the crew and give them cash advances to leave with their families. At the end of the season when all the pearls had been sold, the owner would take half of the total proceeds as profit. The other half was disposed of, firstly by the owner recovering the cost of the food for the season, then deducting a further one fifth as expenses for the boat.

The remainder was strictly divided among the crew so that the captain took two shares, every diver would take one-and-a-half shares, the cook and haulers would take one share each and the boys a-quarter share. Occasionally, the proceeds

ABOVE LEFT: Pearls were very carefully sorted and graded.
ABOVE RIGHT: Seated on rugs laid across the poop deck of a jelbut, a merchant kindly showed me some of his purchases, which included several abnormalities such as large, misshapen pearls and a large, hollow bulbous mass of nacre which he thought might find a home in a museum.
LEFT: Sorting, grading, weighing and valuing pearls.

OVERLEAF: The smiling faces are an obvious indication of how these seafarers are looking forward to being reunited with family and friends – and, of course, their share of profits.

from the sale of the pearls amounted to less than the expenses and the crew would get nothing for their season's work except their food.

The pearls were sorted and graded by pearl merchants according to colour, quality and size and they would often change hands many times before arriving on the Bombay market. From there, they were sent to the world's capitals, particularly to London, Paris and New York. However, at mid-20th century the demand among Western countries for natural pearls had greatly declined, partly for economic reasons and partly because of the cultured-pearl trade. The difference in appearance between cultured and natural pearls was so slight (and usually only detectable by the eye when the cultured pearl had aged) that its introduction into the Arabian Gulf area would have created chaos in the market. For this reason, the cultured pearl was a strictly forbidden import.

The larger pearls were sorted according to colour and the best of them were either white or pink – black and green pearls were not very popular and seldom found a good market. There was a noticeable trend for pink pearls to be more popular in the Nordic countries, where the skin of women was paler, while white pearls were popular in countries where the women's skin was darker.

The story of pearls is a lengthy one which can be only briefly narrated within these few pages but, to my mind, the real romance of the pearl trade lay in the Arabian Gulf during those early pearling days. A natural pearl is a thing of great aesthetic beauty and any woman fortunate to possess a string of them should see in their lustre not the golden guineas with which they were bought, but the time-worn face of a bearded pearler, peering into the silent depths of the sea in search of one of the thousands of pearls which have to be found to select the graded pearls for a small necklace. Sadly, this is yet another of the romantic and ancient crafts that has been lost to the modern world.

LEFT: **After the long pearling season, there was still work to be done! Hulls had to be scraped and oiled and the vessels cleaned and repaired before they were either laid-up for the winter or put into other service. Note the baskets and ropes on which the pearl divers descended.**

PREVIOUS SPREAD: **A pearling vessel at anchorage: Anchors dropped or mooring ropes secured, crowded pearling vessels would come to rest in their home ports.**

ABOVE: Sorting and grading the pearls was a skilled operation.
TOP: Pearl merchants weighing pearls aboard a *jelbut*.
RIGHT: A pearl auction – haggling all the way, recently landed
pearls slowly change hands.

OVERLEAF: Pearl merchants 'skinning' pearls to improve their
shape. This process sometimes took place even while the pearl
was being auctioned, with the bids changing as the shape of
the pearl changed.

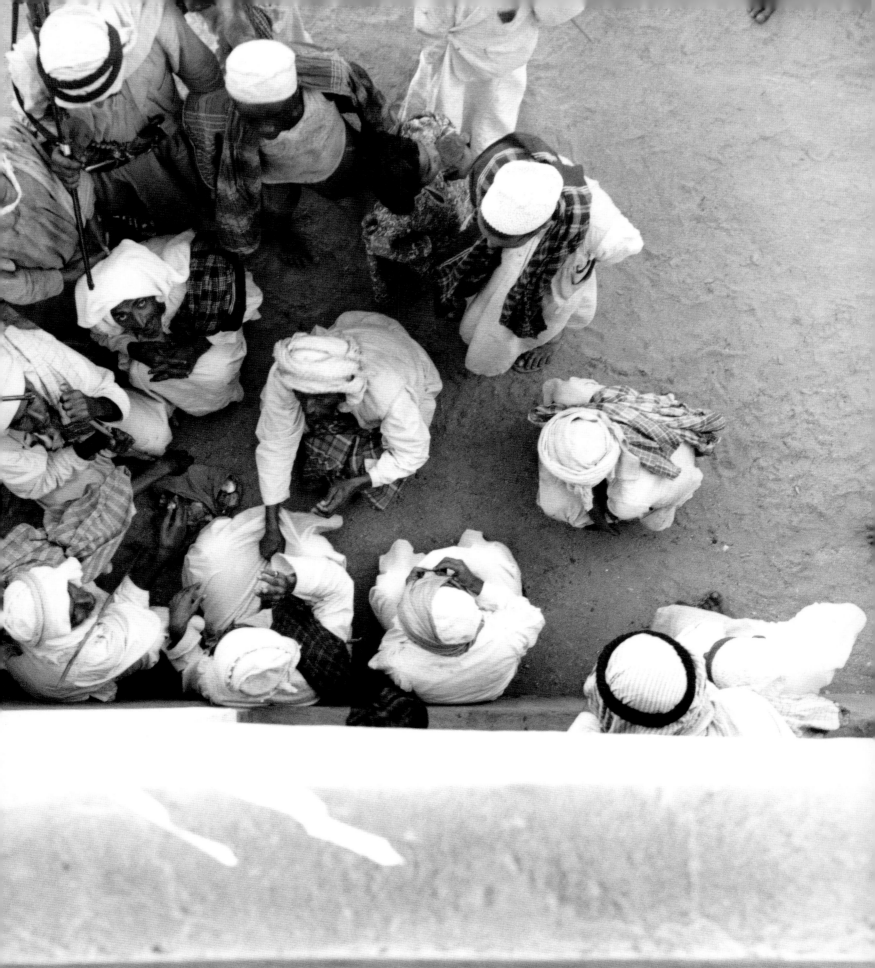

Chapter four

Captains of commerce

Throughout this book, I have used the title *Nakhuda* of a vessel instead of the more familiar 'captain', since the *Nakhuda* was a merchant mariner whose ability to sail and command his vessel was taken for granted. It was his ability as a merchant by which he was judged and, indeed, by which he, his crew and the owners of the vessel were to make a profit.

There were, of course, many vessels that ran from one port to another within the Arabian Gulf carrying cargoes negotiated by the owners, in which case the *Nakhuda* merely acted as a mariner. On the more important and longer trading voyages to Africa and India, however, the *Nakhuda* acted as merchant, broker and agent as well as captaining the vessel.

He was, in effect, a freelance merchant with a floating warehouse at his command. He had to be conversant with the markets and, at any of his ports of call, decide whether to carry another merchant's goods for a fixed price or whether to buy goods and carry them to where he might make a profit – often to the consternation of his crew as this might not be their home port and the voyage would be prolonged. As often as not, his cargo might be a mixture of the two with some fare-paying passengers.

Nawakhid were cast into their role of being men of learning, moulded by their experience, even though they might be illiterate – true learning was born of experience and a clerk could be hired for reading and writing. Their judgment would be sought by passengers and crew to adjudicate in the event of a dispute. In addition, unless the ship

A helmsman, following customary habit, uses his legs to steer the vessel during a long voyage.

carried, as was likely, a self-professed *Muttawaa* (traditional teacher), they might be called on to give guidance and instruction on religious matters.

In my experience, *Nawakhid* were not arrogant, despite the superior role in which they found themselves, and men of greater learning were always welcomed to relieve them of these moral tasks. Seldom, if ever, did they have to lean on their rank to maintain discipline and they relied on

ABOVE: *Bait Al Shamal*, or House of the North Wind – the Ruler's guest-house in Abu Dhabi – as seen from aboard a vessel off the coast. It was some distance from the Ruler's fort, and was mainly used by Bedu from the interior. Whenever the author stayed there, he would find it crowded with Bedu – and their meals would arrive from the fort.

LEFT TOP: Men haul in their nets aboard a small fishing boat off the coast of Ra's al-Khaimah.

LEFT: A view of Sharjah's waterfront as it looked in 1948.

their hard-won and accepted leadership in a livelihood in which only the best survived.

While living in Dubai, I was privileged to meet many *Nawakhid* from whom I learned that the basic management of the vessels, and the role taken by the *Nakhuda*, had changed little through the centuries except for one important innovation – telegraphic communications.

During my time on the Trucial Coast the *Nakhuda*, on reaching his destination or one of his many ports of call, could send a cable to find out about the requirements and prices of commodities on the home market. Prior to this, they would have to guess and gamble.

Even so, despite this ability to communicate by cable, I travelled on vessels on a number of occasions that were hailed by another and enquiries made of the crew as to the availability and prices of goods in certain ports. Armed with this knowledge, the *Nakhuda* would sometimes revise his course and destination. On one such occasion, the reward to the crew of the vessel on which I travelled for the information was a shower of coconuts!

Management of vessels and recruitment of crews was usually in the hands of the *Nakhuda* though, sometimes, the owner of the vessel would conduct these affairs himself and the *Nakhuda*

**ABOVE: A stockpile of *chandals* (mangrove poles) cut from the swamps of the Rufiji Delta in East Africa, piled ashore from the *boom* which had transported them. They were extensively used in the building of coral-stone houses, watch-towers and wind-towers, and as supports for houses made of palm fronds.
RIGHT TOP: A scene at Shindagha – sometimes the shoreline was cluttered with many different types of vessels; at other times, there were none at all.
RIGHT: *Abras* were a notable feature of life, being the main means of crossing the Creek between the three sections of town and of transporting people to vessels anchored away from the shores of the Creek. *Abras* with motors are still in common use today.**

PREVIOUS SPREAD: A waterfront scene on the Creek separating Dubai from Shindagha at high tide. Any vessels not carefully moored would find themselves stranded at low tide.

would act on his instructions. There was an increasing tendency, at mid-century, for crew members to work for a fixed wage, particularly on the internal routes in the Arabian Gulf. However, on the longer voyages, the system of sharing the earnings of the vessel remained much the same as in the past and on the pearling boats. A typical arrangement would be that, from the earnings of the vessel, all its expenses (including the cost of food for the crew) would be deducted and half the balance (the profit) would be paid to the vessel's owner. The remainder would then be divided among the *Nakhuda* and his crew in proportion to the particular job of each member.

I had another experience of the prowess of these merchant mariners while I was exploring a remote pass in the Hajar Mountains that separate the Gulf of Oman from the Arabian Gulf. Turning a bend in a wadi, I unexpectedly came across another party of travellers which had called a mid-day halt on the wadi bed, beneath the ledge on which I was standing. When the guards of our respective parties had satisfied themselves as to the

good intentions of the other, rifles were lowered, greetings exchanged and hospitality offered.

This small party of travellers had succeeded in creating an oasis of luxury in the barren wadi. Colourful carpets were spread over the gravel and, on two sides, the loads from the grazing camels and donkeys had been placed so as to form back-rests. The host at this gathering was the *Nakhuda* of a *Boom*!

The *Nakhuda*'s story of his shipless journey was simple – he was bringing his vessel, laden with a mixed cargo, back from a voyage to Zanzibar and, as a result of various delays, he was one of the last

Left top: The Ruler of Ajman, Sheikh Rashid bin Humaid, arriving at Dubai aboard an *abra*.

Left: A *tawmina* (group of girl graduates from a Koran class), accompanied by their teacher and all dressed up in their best, are rowed across the Creek by *abra*.

Above: An *abra* crosses Dubai Creek with merchant vessels in the background. At the time, there was no formal control of shipping in the Dubai Creek.

of the homeward journeying fleet racing to dispose of their goods in the ports of the Arabian Gulf.

Enquiries he made had brought him the news that the intended market for his goods was poor. At the same time, he had heard of events that had brought a burst of prosperity to a group of oases inland from the coast along which he was travelling. Handing over his ship to his mate, he hired a shore party consisting of guards and pack animals and, taking sacks of spices and some of the less bulky items of his cargo, he embarked on the journey to the interior to find a market for these goods (and, perhaps, to acquire other goods which he could later trade to his advantage).

I shall never know whether it was solely commerce that guided him in the direction he was headed or whether it was a spirit of adventure and enterprise which was so typical of sailors in general, and *Nawakhid* in particular. One thing was apparent from this chance encounter; even ashore, the *Nakhuda* was still in command and his little, temporary camp was very ship-shape!

It was not uncommon to find *Nawakhid* in unexpected situations, often leap-frogging from one vessel to another. Sometimes they would even travel ahead of their own vessels to arrange a cargo, or travel after it, remaining at some port to dispose of a cargo that had been off-loaded, but remained unsold.

The annual trading voyages of the large, ocean-going vessels deserve some special mention. These voyages were based mainly on the monsoon (from the Arabic *Mawsim*) seasons that blew in the Indian Ocean and the routes the vessels took went as far south as the monsoons. A typical voyage would keep a vessel away from its home port for about nine months.

Towards the end of summer, most of these ocean-going vessels would make their way to Basra, where they would load dates. A few of the vessels specialised in rushing to the markets the Oman dates, which ripened earlier than those of Basra. Once loaded, the vessels headed slowly southwards to Cape Musandam, their doorway to the Gulf of

Oman and the Indian and other great oceans and, once in the Indian Ocean, they would run down to Africa on the northeast monsoon. 'Run down' is not, perhaps, the precise term as, during my time in Dubai, the vessels coasted their way along southern Arabia and, from there, down the African coast and rarely crossed the ocean direct.

In the great days of Arab navigators, Gulf craft could be found everywhere in these Eastern Seas. However, the knowledge of mathematics and navigation, at which they excelled, had largely been

Above: Another *abra* man – the fare depended on the number of people traveling together in the boat, eight *annas* being the usual cost of hiring the whole boat for the shortest crossing. Today, at half a dirham, it's still an affordable means of getting around.
Far left: This man of tribal origin – Abdullah bin Mohammed Bel Hasa – was in turn fisherman, pearler, mariner and then boat owner. He is smoking a tiny pipe of the type used by the Bedu which, together with a small tin of dry, crumbled tobacco, he kept in the pocket of his *sidairi* (waistcoat), a garment worn over the *thaub* and very popular because of the usefulness of its pockets.
Left: An *abra* man (ferryman) in Dubai.

lost. (Evidence that astral navigation was familiar to the early Arabs is found in the *Koran*, Sura VI (97) – "And He it is Who hath set for you the stars that ye may guide your course by them amid the darkness of the land or sea. We have detailed our revelations for a people who have knowledge.") Bearings on the sun were taken at mid-day and, apart from this one check on their position, most vessels coasted and, in the most uncanny fashion, the sailors simply seemed to know the way.

Each vessel carried on age-old trading activities, buying and selling merchandise as they went. Among the cargoes carried were dates, shark's meat and other dried fish, shark's oil, ivory, coffee, frankincense, myrrh, rice, Indian corn, sugar, tinned milk and other tinned foods, timber, coconuts and coconut fibre, ghee and cooking oils, cotton, tobacco, honey, cloves, copra, lemons, limes, sesame seeds and all varieties of spices; in short, any commodity whatsoever that was likely to be in demand and which would show a profit.

Pearls were among the most valuable cargo carried in these vessels but, at mid-century, they were mostly taken by the merchants by steamer to Bombay or flown direct to the world's markets.

If the voyage from the Trucial Coast was to Zanzibar, Mombasa or one of the other East African ports, then the *Nakhuda* would have to decide on whether to buy a return cargo of *chandals* (mangrove poles from the swamps of East Africa which were used for building and were usually a profitable cargo for the Arabian Gulf – many an old house in the Trucial States had its architecture determined by the size of these poles) or whether to reduce his costs by obtaining a licence to take his vessel into such places as the Rufiji Delta (300 miles south of Zanzibar) to cut his own poles from the swamp. It was known as the 'Delta of Misery' and no one liked going into those mosquito swamps – the crew would, therefore, have to be paid an incentive to withstand the severe hardship of those trips. Once they were

The *Nakhuda* checks his sails. The crew carried out their tasks with a minimum of orders, instinctively knowing what had to be done. Fearlessly, they regarded the climbing of a mast or into the often-precarious rigging as being no more than climbing a palm tree. Such accidents as did occur were more likely to be caused by worn rigging than over-confidence or lack of respect for the sea, and repairs to the hull, sails and rigging were a constant task.

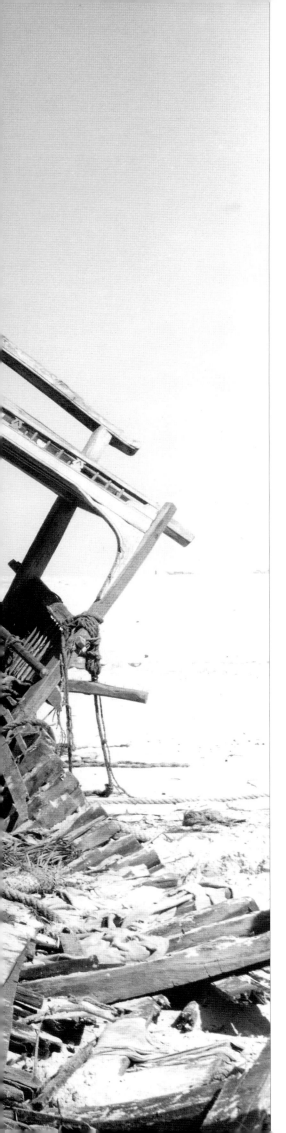

there, everyone's mission was to cut their cargo and get out again as quickly as possible.

When merchants had freight to send on these vessels, they usually paid the charges on each bale or package and preferred not to charter the vessel as this was not the best incentive to keep a crew out of harbour.

With the inheritance of well-proven sailing craft, the seafarers of the Trucial Coast were natural sailors, although the driving force behind their adventurous existence was their trading activities. If you've ever wondered why the spirit of free enterprise is so prevalent in the Emirates today, you need look no further than the activities of the *Nawakhid* through the centuries, up to the recent past, to find the answer. Trading activities were so much a part of daily existence in the ports along the Trucial Coast that that spirit has become ingrained – and still lives on in modern times.

ABOVE: All hands on deck – here, the *Nakhuda* assists his crew to haul in the mainsail.
LEFT: The shipwreck of a Bahraini craft on Jumeirah Beach – many lives were lost every year in shipwrecks but at the time there was no news media to record such tragedies. Eleven lives were lost in this wreck. Here the *Nakhuda* is seen atop the boat's twisted poop, surveying the damage.

Chapter five

Shipbuilding

The Trucial States did not produce timber suitable for building large ships, nor iron for nails. This made the early growth of the seafaring tradition in the Arabian Gulf, and around the shores of Jezirat Al 'Arab, all the more surprising.

It is probable that the earliest attempts in the Arabian Gulf to build sea-going craft were made by tying together the stems of palm fronds with palm fibres. I saw such a craft, called a *shasha*, in the shape of a canoe about 12-feet long and large enough for two men, still in use on the coast of Fujairah, the palm fibre having been soaked in fish oil. More widely used, but also of antiquity, was the *hoori*, a canoe dug out of a single tree.

In later times when wood (but not iron for nails) became available, boats were made by stitching together the timbers with a giant needle and cord. Evidence of this was still occasionally seen along the Trucial Coast when I lived there. Fragile though these craft must have been, they were the early foundation on which the development of the vessels and, indeed, the seafaring tradition of the Trucial States, was built.

Abu Zaid Hasan, an Arab writer of the 10th century, gives this interesting account of shipbuilding in his times :

"There are people, at 'Oman', who cross over to the islands that produce the Coco-nut, carrying with them carpenter's and such-like Tools; and having felled as much wood as they want, they let it dry, then strip off the leaves, and with the Bark of the Tree they spin a Yarn, wherewith they sew the Planks together, and so

Sailmakers from Shindagha at work on a lateen sail staked out on a flat area of sand at Khabaiba. Although it was difficult toiling in the hot, bright sun, the work had to be done.

build a ship. Of the same wood they cut and round away a mast; of the Leaves they weave their Sails, and the Bark they make into Cordage. Having thus completed their Vessel, they load her with Coco-nuts, which they bring and sell at 'Oman'. Thus it is that, from this Tree alone, so many Articles are convertible to use, as suffice not only to build and rig out a vessel, but to load her when she is completed, and in a Trim to sail."

What more could any mariner desire – even of a tree! But lest the reader is led to believe that these mariners sailed on the Seas of Paradise, it would be as well to give the other side of the story. In the words of Marco Polo (some two centuries after Abu Zaid):

"Their ships are wretched affairs, and many of them get lost; for they have no iron fastening, and they are only stitched together with twine made from the husk of the Indian nut. They beat the husk until it becomes like horse-hair, and from that they spin a twine, and with this stitch the planks of the ships together. It keeps well, and is not corroded by the seawater, but will not stand well in a storm. The ships are not pitched, but are rubbed with fish oil. They have one mast, one sail, and one rudder, and have no deck, but only a cover spread over the cargo when loaded. This consists of hides, and on top of these hides they put the horses which they take to India for sale. They have no iron to make nails of, and for this reason, they use only wooden trenails in their shipbuilding, and then stitch the planks with twine as I have told you. Hence 'tis a perilous business to go a voyage in one of these ships, and many of them are lost, for in that Sea of India the storms are often terrible."

(Here it is worth mentioning that although western history gives credit to Polo for opening the trade route to China, Arabs were engaged in trade with that part of the world at least 500 years earlier.)

Flimsy though the craft may have been (which, in itself, gave them ease of handling and flexibility denied to larger, sturdier vessels), not so the men who sailed them. In the words of that legendary 10th-century character, Sindbad:

" . . . where I found a great ship already filled with honest, goodhearted merchants of the kind who can live contentedly together and render aid when aid is needed. I embarked with them in the vessel, and we at once set sail, with the blessing of Allah upon our voyage. . . ."

In later times, as suitable materials became available for shipbuilding, the development of a vessel that has survived to this day was begun. All their seafaring experience and knowledge of shipbuilding was incorporated into the basic design

ABOVE: The adze was used to shape masts from a tree trunk that could be more than 90-feet long.

TOP: A sailmaker at work on a flat area of ground.

LEFT: A vessel damaged during a storm is beached for repairs at Madhaif, near Khorfakkan, supported by a few *chandals*.

OVERLEAF: Builders of traditional craft in the Gulf used few tools, the principal two being the adze and the Indian (bow) drill.

of their vessels and in the many different types of craft that have evolved from it. The two main features of the design are the lateen rig and the shallow hull which is so essential for the shallow waters on the Arabian side of the Gulf. The success of this design is the story of its long survival – through the centuries – to modern times.

Each type of vessel has its own name and the main collective, or general term, for them all in Arabic is *khashab,* meaning timbers. I have avoided using the more familiar, but incorrect, name 'dhows' though, in itself, it is worthy of mention. Europeans used it believing it to be an Arabic word; Arabs, who were in contact with Europeans, heard it used so frequently that they assimilated it, believing it to be English!

The real origin of the word remains something of a mystery but, from my investigations, I am led to believe that the dhow was a type of large sailing vessel (similar in appearance to a *baghala*) used for warfare which was mainly, or solely, used from Muscat and Oman on long journeys to Africa. If this is correct, then the dhow may well have been the craft which the Omanis used when driving the Portuguese from Zanzibar, which they later colonised. But the mistaken use of the word

continues, veiling more heavily its origin. Perhaps a time will be reached when it will have been absorbed into both Arabic and English as the only generally accepted name for Arab sailing vessels.

The vessels of the Emirates are remarkable for the beauty of their lines and the gracefulness of their curves. At various times in history, there have been as many as a score of different types of craft and, while there are similarities in the fleet as a whole, to the casual observer there is no apparent difference between some of the types. They differ in size, rig, shape of stern and length of keel in proportion to their total length, while other slight differences (somewhat easier for laypeople to recognise) are maintained in connection with the formation of stem and stern-post heads and in the decorative styles displayed on them.

In former times, the different types of craft

ABOVE: A *jelbut* **hauled ashore for repairs on the banks of Dubai Creek (note the palm-frond shelter over the poop deck). The sandy area would flood at high tide.**
RIGHT: In areas of strong currents, any sandy shore was used to beach craft for repairs and maintenance. Here, in Ajman, an ancient craft overlooks more modern equipment.

were often the speciality of different ports, but this was no longer true of the larger craft and it was only the smaller, mainly fishing, boats which retained features of their ports of origin. Kuwait was always regarded as the leading centre for shipbuilding in the Arabian Gulf – one of the reasons given for this was that the relatively dry climate there seasoned the wood better than elsewhere in the Gulf. However, this reasoning did not appear entirely valid as Bahrain, Sur and many other ports produced equally good vessels despite suffering the most humid of climates.

Here follows a brief description of the main types of craft, most of which are well illustrated in this book.

Traditionally, the *baghala* was a deep-sea, cargo-carrying craft of the Arabian Gulf, although almost extinct during my time in Dubai. During the heyday of this type of craft, the largest were said to have been up to 120 to 130 feet in length, carrying a crew of up to 100 men and a cargo of from 300 to 500 tons. The last of them were much smaller. The most distinguishing feature of the *baghala* was its elaborately-carved stern and windowed quarter-

galleries which, although picturesque, were apt to be dangerous in a pounding sea. Its stem-piece was a simple, up-turned square, surrounded by a circular centre piece.

The *Boom* took the place of the *Baghala* and was the largest craft built in the Arabian Gulf. It was of varying sizes, the smallest of which were used as lighters in port and on short voyages, while the biggest were the ocean-going vessels that journeyed to Africa and India. As with most of the other types of craft, the *Boom* was easily distinguished by its stem-piece which took the form of a long, planked, built-up bowsprit as long

Left and above: The curve of the Creek at which Shindagha was separated from Dubai was a popular place for sailors to beach their craft for repairs and maintenance.

Overleaf: Made entirely from parts of the palm tree, the ancient *shasha* was around 10- to 12-feet long and carried one or two fishermen. It soon became waterlogged and heavy and required several helpers to haul it back onto the beach where it was left to dry in the sun.

as 20 feet, usually painted and ringed at the end. Its stern was pointed, almost like the bow, and it was this feature that was said to make it a faster and better sea-boat than the *baghala*, particularly in a following sea. The largest *booms* were said to carry up to 300 tons of cargo.

The *sambuq* was one of the best-known types of Arab sailing craft. It established a reputation for itself as being a good pearling boat (the *boom* was rarely used for this purpose), mainly for the ease with which it could be rowed at the pearling banks. It was, in fact, a very good all-rounder that was used for pearling, fishing, lightering and as a good cargo carrier, varying in size from a small, open boat to a medium-sized, fully-decked craft. It had a fairly low, curved stem, and a high, square stern.

Jelbut is a name believed to have originated from the English 'jolly-boat', although the Portuguese *galliot* (galley) and Indian *gallevat* have also been suggested, since *jelbut* is sometimes pronounced *jalibut*. In the past, this craft was used mainly for pearling, fishing and as a small cargo-cum-passenger vessel, but it came into its own when it was found to be the easiest craft in which

to fit a marine engine. It was frequently called *launch* in Arabic (plural *launchat*). It was distinguished by its straight, upright bow and transom stern.

The *shu'ai* was a small version of the *sambuq*, used extensively for pearling and fishing. Its stem-piece differed from that of the *sambuq* in the manner in which it was built up.

The *mashuwah* was a small craft used mainly for fishing or carrying small cargoes. *mashuwah* was also used as a general term for a longboat which was either rowed or sometimes rigged.

Among the other types were the *batil, bagara, kutiyah, ghunchah* (a small type of *baghala*), *dangi, zaruga* and *khansha*.

(I should point out that the estimates of cargo

LEFT: A *baggarah* fishing off the coast of Ra's al-Khaimah. These attractive and distinctive high-sterned craft were used mainly in the waters of the Gulf of Oman.

ABOVE AND OVERLEAF: Fishermen tend to their nets in and beside another *baggarah*. Behind them lies the Hajar Mountains.

capacity I have used are only very approximate as, enterprisingly, baskets of dates, each about 180 pounds in weight, were the yardstick used to measure the vessels' capacity.)

A large Arab sailing vessel at sea was a sight to stir the emotions of anyone with a sentiment for old sailing ships as its forward-raking mainmast, its mizzenmast raking the other way, its high, galleon-like poop and the graceful droop of its waist were all classic, timeless features. But it was something of a shock to see the simple tools and rule-of-thumb methods used in the construction of these craft. However, the entire process of building became a joy to behold when you saw a shapely hulk being created from a pile of logs.

The shipwright possessed a few saws, a rough plane or two and an Indian drill; his bare feet he used as a vice and his most frequently used tool was the adze. His greatest aid was the experience passed down through the centuries and his skill acquired through long apprenticeship; the plans were in his head as he had no drawings or blueprints to guide him.

The vessels were constructed on the beaches near the high-water mark so that they could be launched by heaving them sideways into the water. The shipbuilder gave his ships plenty of good ribs and they took on a beautiful symmetry at the

LEFT AND ABOVE: The *boom* was the most popular – and most widely used – of the large, load-carrying sailing craft in the Arabian Gulf and Indian Ocean. Many were owned by Dubai merchants but some called at Dubai while sailing under the flags of other Trucial and Gulf states.

115

ABOVE: The characteristic stem head or *satur* (always painted with a black tip and a white line) immediately identifies this traditional craft as a *boom*.

RIGHT TOP AND BOTTOM: There was no formal control of shipping in Dubai's Creek and craft such as these *booms* were anchored at convenient positions for loading and unloading cargo.

OVERLEAF: A *boom* at anchor in Dubai Creek – those requiring maintenance or repair were anchored where they would be conveniently exposed at low tide.

hands of the craftsmen, resulting in vessels that were well put together. The hulls were of roughly adzed planks fastened to the ribs by trenails and the seams of the planking were caulked with raw cotton. The mainmast, which might rise some 90 feet above the sea, was shaped from a single tree. A large lateen yard, however, would be made from the trunks of three trees stoutly lashed together with canvas and bound with rope. Large craft were nearly all decked and given suitable hatchways.

Before launching, the outside of the hull would

be coated, to prevent fouling, with a mixture of whitewash and grease boiled together while the remainder of the ship was coated with sharks' oil to prevent the timbers from warping. These coatings were usually renewed about twice a year.

A new vessel was given a name by its owner or newly appointed *Nakhuda* – *Fat Al Khair, Dar Al Salaam, Suheil, Tharaya* and *Ghannas* being a few of the names I can remember of the vessels in which I travelled. A new crew was formed and, after a simple fitting-out, the vessel was ready for launching and for a few trials before its first voyage.

The launching, whether of a new craft or a vessel that had been beached for cleaning, was a boisterous affair in which the crews of many vessels gave a hand. Loudly chanting, sometimes to the accompaniment of the beat of a drum (as when hoisting sails at sea), the vessel was heaved and levered into the water until a great cheer proclaimed her afloat. The sailors had a chant, or sea shanty, for every occasion and task which they repeated many times until the task in hand was completed. It might be a short ballad of some

recent happening or, heavy-hearted at leaving port, they might be heard singing this refrain as they hauled up the anchor and hoisted the great sail until their voices were lost in the great expanse of sea that was their true home:

"We are going, and depend on God,
Our lover, the Prophet,
Our lover, God the King – forever good morning!
The West wind has turned – hoist a sail."

RIGHT: A large, unladen *sambuq* moored off Shindagha.
ABOVE: A large *sambuq* waiting for the tide in Dubai Creek. Even at high tide it was not always possible to cross 'The Bar' if a strong wind was blowing or a heavy sea running. Conversely, in a complete calm, it might have to be 'poled' or towed across by its crew rowing a longboat.

OVERLEAF: *Sambuqs* were of varying sizes; the smaller craft were frequently used as pearling boats while the larger craft (together with the *boom*) were popular as load carriers.

A *jelbut* sails into Dubai Creek with Shindagha in the
background. These craft were said to have taken their name
from the English 'jollyboat' or Indian *gallevat* which, in turn,
was said to have derived from the Portuguese for 'galley'.

Jelbuts beached for maintenance on the shores of the Creek near Bury Khalifa. Most vessels that entered the Creek were of the shallower draft *jelbut* or *sambuq* type – as the larger *booms* could barely enter when fully laden.

**Two *jelbuts* make a stirring sight as they race for home on calm
seas. Note the beautiful trim of the leading boat.**

**The waters of the Gulf were often calm but this also meant
there was often less wind than would have been preferred.**

ABOVE AND LEFT BELOW: The *jelbut* was the most suitable of the many traditional types of wooden-hulled sailing craft for motorising and, when fitted with an engine, became known in Arabic as *launch*. At first the motorised *jelbuts* retained their masts but these were eventually discarded by craft used for local ferrying. They were however ideal craft for operating in shallow waters, drawing around three feet of water.

LEFT TOP: Owned by a well-known seafarer and contractor, Khan Sahib Hussain Amad (who was HMG's Resident Agent in Sharjah in 1935), this was one of the first *jelbuts* to be fitted with a diesel engine. Named the *Qannas* (the hunter), it was little more than 30-feet long and small for its type. It is shown here surveying channels through shallow waters with its *Nakhuda* standing on the awning over the poop deck for the best view.

LEFT, ABOVE AND PREVIOUS SPREAD: **This magnificent *kutiyah*, on its homeward voyage to Dubai, carried a cargo of *chandals*, spices and cloth. Nearing port, the vessel had been away for a 10-month round-trip voyage to Africa; on the outward voyage it had carried a cargo of dates from Basra.**

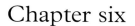

Chapter six

Life afloat

In many ways, the customs and way of life of the sailors aboard ship were similar to those of the Bedu of the desert except in one basic respect: the Bedu is probably one of the most independent of people in the world, whereas the sailor has to adapt to fit in as a member of a crew. Even so, this difference was not immediately obvious to anyone travelling aboard a strange ship, surrounded by unfamiliar faces.

On-board routine was carried out in the most informal manner: there were no routine watches, no logs, no drill and no formal 'going below' as all hands lived and slept on deck. The crew would see what had to be done and they would do it and, consequently, very few orders were given. Yet, beneath this happy-go-lucky façade, there was an orderliness and discipline as strong and rugged as on any vessel afloat.

The size of the crew naturally differed with the size and type of vessel, although the organisation was basically the same for all. Moreover, the number of seamen and supernumaries employed on vessels of the same type varied considerably. A typical crew of a large ocean-going *boom* might be: one *Nakhuda* (the merchant master), one *mu'allim* (mate, or principle officer), three *skkanis* (helmsmen, who usually assist in sail-making), one or two *tabbakhs* and assistants (cooks and general hands), one *sarhang* (boatswain), 10 to 20 *bahriyah* (sailors) and perhaps, on long trading voyages, a *qurrani* (clerk).

Most trading vessels carried passengers, often a considerable number, and it was only after the vessel had been at sea for some time that the unacquainted passenger would be able to distinguish deckhands from passengers. Many of

135

the passengers would be busily engaged in trading activities between the sailors or other passengers, sometimes establishing small canteens to cater for themselves and others who were travelling at a cheaper fare, which did not include food. An emergency at sea was, perhaps, the quickest way of discerning sailors from passengers as the crew would swing on ropes over the heads of the passengers to reach their duty stations. Such an occurrence also demonstrated the effectiveness of the crew organisation.

As the vessel made her way through the sea, the quiet of her isolation among the waves would be broken only by voices – there were no bells to sound the watches, no whistles to give rise to orders yet, in this atmosphere of considerable informality, the crew would go about their tasks with an air of confidence that came from being born into a life at sea. The sun was the only timepiece that mattered.

When the stars faded, the sleeping members of the crew would begin to stir and the captain would descend from his bed on the navigators' bench high across the stern to perform the dawn prayers. Like the Bedu of the desert, most sailors preferred to pray individually rather than in line. The helmsman and lookout would be relieved of their posts and the *Nakhuda* would call for his breakfast which, as for the crew, usually consisted of sweet tea without milk, unleavened bread and, as a luxury, vermicelli, followed by bitter coffee.

A charming feature of social life in the desert was that, after prayers, even people who had been continuously together for long periods made a point of greeting each other; at sea, the custom was the same. One by one, members of the crew would walk onto the poop-deck, raise their hands in greeting to whomever was there and wish everyone a good morning.

During the morning the decks, if they were not crowded with passengers, would be washed down and the crew would carry out any repairs to the sails or riggings that were necessary. On a long voyage, to while away the hours, it might be that the ship's carpenter, assisted by one or two of the deckhands, would build a small boat which he would sell at one of the ports of call. Sometimes, a

Sailors in the rigging of a vessel – unfortunately, accidents could (and did) happen at sea. This photograph gives some idea of the sheer scale of the task.

137

ABOVE: Sailing offshore of Dubai – and most probably carrying an interesting variety of wares. The needs and prices of goods required at the different ports were usually a bit of a guess and gamble and these vessels would even exchange notes at sea.

RIGHT TOP AND BOTTOM: Clambering about the boat – but these sailors knew, from years of experience, exactly what to do.

small group might be engaged in building crudely-made, but attractive, model boats for sale. Sailors sometimes set about hammering brass studs into heavy wooden chests, thereby making elaborate patterns on them – the 'Kuwaiti' and *Suri* types of chest are probably the most famous, although similar chests would be made by sailors from ports all over the Gulf.

Those crew engaged in private trading activities might also be busy rebottling perfumes or otherwise preparing their wares for sale. However,

ABOVE: Socotri, a well-known Dubai sailor. Strong, cheerful and highly experienced, he took his name from his place of birth, Socotra, in the Gulf of Aden, where as a small boy he had joined a vessel from Dubai.

TOP: This mariner, who had journeyed under sail between the Gulf and East India, scrutinises the deceptively calm horizon. This photograph was taken offshore of Dubai.

LEFT: A helmsman steering with his leg – a common practice.

during a long voyage, all was not private enterprise for the sailors and an almost endless task for the benefit of the vessel was the laying-up of cables made from coconut fibre (*kair-coir*) from India and, of course, the sewing of sails.

Cooking was done on a wood or charcoal fire in an enclosed fire-box. The mess arrangements for the crew were simple, though naturally they differed in standard according to the prosperity of a particular trading voyage and the taste and temperament of the *Nakhuda*. Coffee, tea, rice, dates, flour and sugar were the staple provisions. According to the status of the vessel, the rice would be embellished with either fresh or dried fish and, on very rare occasions, meat. Tinned foods added variety to the mess and enhanced special occasions. Lentils, curry powder, onions, cardamom and other spices were among the other provisions carried when finances permitted and fresh limes, which the sailors wisely stocked up on whenever available, were squeezed with great relish over rice and fish.

Passengers who were seasick would lie huddled about the decks with wads of cotton stuffed up their nostrils which they occasionally removed to sniff at a lime or lemon, this being the generally accepted cure for seasickness. This perpetuated a belief of the Bedu that many illnesses came from odours; hence the cotton wads.

Fresh water was carried in large, wooden tanks, and many a vessel on a long trading voyage had to alter course and make for the nearest port when her water supply gave out. Unhappy was the voyage during which the crew had to subsist on brackish, sulphurous or otherwise polluted water. This might be because there was no other choice at the last port of call or because some water vendor had cheated them and drawn water from the poorest wells.

The sailors had a song or a chant for every occasion and for every major task such as hoisting the main sail, refloating the vessel after beaching or hauling up the anchor (a task in which sailors from

ABOVE: A mariner at rest, offshore of Abu Dhabi.
LEFT: A sailor rests at the bow of a *jelbut* approaching the rugged coast of Ra's al-Khaimah.

other vessels might lend a hand). The solemn and slow beat of a drum would keep the rhythm.

Entering a port, particularly after a long voyage, could be a showy business and the vessel would either be brought in under tow by many oars from its longboat full of chanting sailors or it would be brought in under sail. The latter was often dramatic to watch as, sometimes, in the excitement of reaching port, the *Nakhuda* would adopt a dare-devil attitude and bring in his vessel at speed, turning it into the wind at the last moment.

It was not unusual to see sailors diving overboard with lines to attach to other vessels to arrest their vessel's movement and, if this operation was done badly, to hear vessels in a crowded port bumping into one another as they received the

shock of the newcomer. The most impressive arrival, although the practice had declined, was where the crew would gather in the bows when their vessel arrived at a strange village or town. Then, with their hands cupped, they would loudly and slowly chorus the greeting, "*Salaam Alaikum*".

The zenith of social life was reached when the ship was in port for several days where there were other vessels at anchor and visits could be

ABOVE: **Homeward bound to Dubai from the east coast of Africa – a long and arduous double crossing.**
LEFT: **With sails trimmed but still at anchor, this vessel was waiting for high tide so as to be able to sail across 'The Bar' at the entrance to Dubai Creek.**

exchanged by the crews. Carpets were placed on the poop, surrounded by cushions and the decorated chests of the sailors, and an awning fixed overhead. The sailors would squat before their tiny mirrors grooming themselves for their visits ashore and to the other vessels. Fresh meats, and other delicacies unavailable at sea, were obtained and relished.

High-spirited sailors would seek out old and new friends from among the other crews with whom they would spend their leisure time

chatting, reminiscing and exchanging news – the coffee pots and tea kettles would be working overtime. Lucky was the vessel that could boast an instrumentalist as then, by the light of hurricane lamps, the songs of happy sailors would penetrate the night long after darkness until silence finally closed in around the other vessels. The sailor's life was a hard one but there were moments such as these when the companionship of other men lessened the severity of the environment.

When their vessels were in port, however, all

was not leisure and pleasure for the sailors. Cargoes had to be negotiated and disposed of and, if the stay was of any duration, the vessel might have to be beached for repairs or cleaning. The sails were strong, but often badly sewn ("better to lose a sail than a good mast") and frequently needed attention or renewing. A flat piece of ground near an anchorage usually had one or two sails pegged out on it ready for sewing.

At the end of the voyage, when the vessel was laid-up in her home port, not all the crew were

ABOVE: This *kutiyah* is on its homeward voyage to Dubai, laden with a cargo of *chandals*. On its outward voyage, it had carried a cargo of dates from Basra.
LEFT: Sailing home from Africa – Arabs have always been a prominent seafaring people.

OVERLEAF: Waiting for the high tide in Dubai Creek.

retained for maintenance and repair work and many filled in their time until the next voyage by once again seeking their fortune from pearl-diving.

These, then, were the great grandsons of Sindibad (if, as was thought, his origin was Sind, the Indian port of considerable importance as an emporium for Arab trade, his name would be 'Sindibad' rather than the more widely used 'Sindbad' or even 'Sinbad'), the merchant adventurer of *The Thousand and One Nights*, whose name will forever be linked with this ancient and picturesque seafaring trade which, for the most part, was the same during my time in the Gulf as it was when the tales of Sindibad were born in the ninth and 10th centuries.

RIGHT: Waiting for the tide was a regular occurrence – and frustration – before a voyage.
ABOVE: A great grandson of Sindibad – born into their calling, the mariners of the Arabian Gulf were the aristocrats of the sea, upholders of a long seafaring tradition, just as the Bedu were the aristocrats of the sands.

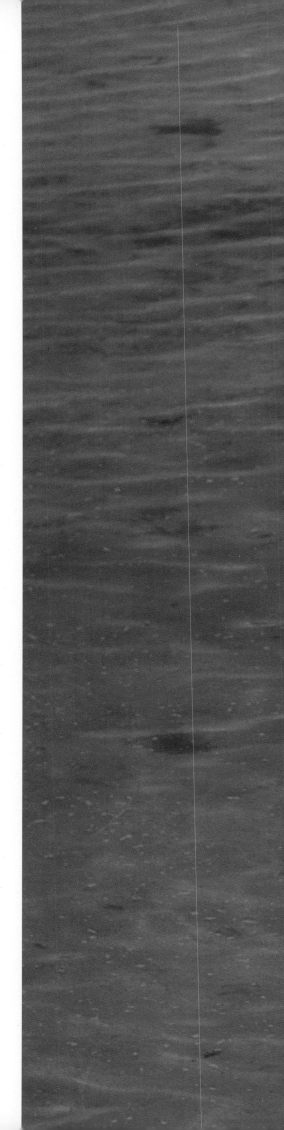

RIGHT: Mariners in the making – the hulls of these model sailing craft were enterprisingly shaped from discarded petrol tins, the masts from camel sticks and the sails from pieces of discarded *wazars* (loincloths).

ABOVE: Young girls admire a model *boom* – this model was made by a member of the crew of a *boom* on its return voyage from Africa to the Gulf. Another pastime of sailors on long voyages was to hammer brass studs into teak-wood chests (at the time, usually known as Kuwaiti chests).

Chapter seven

Mariners' tales

The sailors of the Arabian Gulf had a large repertoire of seafaring stories, some of which were versions of the tales of Sindibad from *The Thousand and One Nights* that had been passed down through the centuries, from mouth to mouth, until only the basic structure of the story remained unchanged. The Arabian Gulf was the setting for many of these tales of Sindibad and, whenever I sighted a whale (usually somewhere about the Straits of Hormuz or in the Gulf of Oman), I recalled Sindibad's landing on the 'strange island' that led to some of his adventures.

But, in truth, the sailors spent little time on storytelling; most of their conversations were taken up with more factual sea talk and recollected details of particular voyages and trading deals. There were more material topics than in the past and, as a result, storytelling had become a declining art. True stories and adventures were more in vogue than the embroidered fantasies of fiction.

One such story was recounted to me by a serious-faced *Nakhuda* in Dubai, an introspective person who was forever trying to interpret the most ordinary happenings as omens of good or evil. He claimed that the events he related happened to him personally, less than 20 years prior to my encounter with him.

Returning from a long, African voyage, the *Nakhuda's* vessel was on course for Bahrain, with the Straits of Hormuz one day behind. It was a warm, humid evening and the vessel was becalmed on a smooth sea. The end of the great lateen sail was drooped over the deck on which many passengers were spread about, listlessly trying to sleep in the humid, still atmosphere while the

The shipwreck of a Bahraini craft on Jumeirah Beach, with people surveying the damage and salvaging whatever could be recycled – nothing in this barren area was left to waste.

vessel drifted beneath the stars. Then, suddenly, a single puff of air travelled across the water, disturbing the tranquillity of the night. The gust momentarily billowed the great sail before releasing it to fall back on to the deck, but the scene it left in its wake was vastly different to the peace it had disturbed. The events that followed were ample justification for any sailor to believe the squall was the cloak of a *jinn*.

With the passing of the squall, the end of the great sail was dragged across some of the passengers. Those who slept on were soon awakened by the screams of a woman. "My child, my child", she screamed, "he's been swept overboard!" The vessel was soon in an uproar: there was no time for enquiries, even had they been possible above the tumult of voices. The longboat was quickly lowered, a lantern was lit and the oarsmen rowed around the vessel in the darkness, searching the water. Aboard the vessel a group of passengers tried to pacify the wailing mother.

Many minutes passed while the search was in progress until, suddenly, there was another cry from the mother, this time in a different pitch. She had found her child where she had safely lodged him for the night: in a coil of rope!

The *Nakhuda* called out to the oarsmen to return and, as he did so, his call was met with a muffled, indiscernible reply. The longboat came alongside and the sailors raised on to the deck of the vessel a dripping body, then held the lantern above the face. It was the face of a wizened, grey-bearded old man – the light from the lantern made pearls from the globules of water that ran down his face and beard. He was dead, but his body was still warm, suggesting that he had not long expired.

People die and, once dead, it makes no difference whether their graves are at sea or in the sand; none were more aware of this than the fatalistic sailors. Yet now the *Nakhuda* and crew stood around the corpse, silent and bewildered, their fears beginning to unfurl like sails. The face before them was unknown; the man was neither a member of the crew nor a passenger. At sunset that night, no other vessel had been in sight. "From where had this old man come to die?": that was a question the *Nakhuda* and his crew asked many times as they sat in the coffee shops of the many ports they later visited, relating their story and describing, in vain, the wizened old man whom nobody seemed to know.

Well may you be incredulous and find this incident hard to believe. Some might suggest that the corpse had washed from some shore or out-of-

ABOVE: Another view of the shipwreck on Jumeirah Beach – in 1950 alone, more than 200 people were lost during storms.
LEFT: The sea took a heavy toll at the entrance to Dubai Creek. A sand-bar guarded the entrance to each of the inlets (*khors*) on which most of the principal towns of the Trucial Coast were situated. In earlier times, shallow-draft vessels were able to navigate these barriers, while pursuing British vessels were forced to remain at sea. The channels through these sand-bars were constantly silting and changing, but the more experienced *Nawakhid* could manage to safely navigate their sailing craft through the shallows, although occasionally one would come to grief, driven on to a bar by a strong *shamal*, the prevailing northwesterly wind. This *boom*, heavily laden with cargo, was one of the unfortunates that didn't make it.

sight vessel and that the crew were mistaken about its warmth. There could be many explanations, but none of them account for the extraordinary coincidence of the event that caused the sailors to search the sea – at that place and exactly that time.

By way of contrast, some efforts of the mariners were devoted to avoiding the possibility of any strange occurrences. These actions were based on superstitions but, at some point, obviously had their basis in fact and must have related to an actual incident. Who is to know? To best illustrate the point, I shall relate an encounter I had with a night-watchman on a beach in Dubai.

The retreating shadows of sunset crept slowly along the shores of Dubai, forming weird shapes around ordinary objects. One of these objects was the wooden hulk of a large sailing craft, hauled up on the beach for repair; its one side warmed by the reddened sunlight, its other casting a shadow over the skeleton of a newly-laid keel, embracing it as though an offspring.

In the shadow, a patient figure sat beside the ribbed keel awaiting the last rays that would herald the evening prayers. Beside him, resting on the embers of a small fire, was the coffee pot that was to be his only companion throughout his night-long vigil beneath the stars. This squatting figure was no mere night-watchman – he was, in his own words, the guardian of a human life, a life that might well have been his own when he had roamed that great desert, the sea.

Sailors had good reason to believe that they were not masters of their own destinies and one of the beliefs, among the seafaring people along the shores of the Arabian Gulf, was that if a barren woman jumped over a newly-laid keel she would conceive. The *jinns*, however, the weavers of misfortune, are not merciful and the woman can only conceive on the basis of a life for a life – the life of the *Nakhuda* or a member of the crew of the new vessel must be forfeit.

And so it was that the wizened ex-sailor sat on guard over the new keel – to ensure that no child-starved woman should steal a life.

PREVIOUS SPREAD: Another victim succumbs to the relentless waves of the Gulf Coast.

RIGHT: An armed tribesman on watch over Khorfakkan in the Musandam Peninsula.

Al akus

Around the middle of the century, a camera was still a rare sight in southeastern Arabia and, when I photographed them, many of my subjects were seeing one for the first time. Imaginatively, both camera and photographs were aptly referred to as *al akus*, meaning 'reflections'.

Considering the extent to which people in the region had been isolated from such modern innovations, they were exceedingly tolerant of the strange object pointed in their direction. In part, this may have been due to the fact that I always tried to maintain an acceptable standard of etiquette when photographing, without which the camera can be an unwelcome intrusion into privacy. As far as circumstances would permit, and without too much loss of spontaneity, I either sought permission before photographing, or tried to get my subjects interested in what I was doing by letting them look through the camera's viewfinder – a novel and amusing experience for most. Thanks largely to the good nature of the people I was photographing or travelling with, my photographic endeavours have invariably been shared experiences, pleasurable to me and entertaining to others.

Whenever possible, I later showed the results to those I photographed but, on the whole, my subjects were usually more interested in obtaining one of my screw-top film canisters in which to keep finely-chopped local tobacco for their tiny pipes, than they were in the photographs. More photographs resulted in more canisters, so photography was very popular indeed!

During the early post-war years there was a dearth of photographic equipment on the market, and most cameras were expensive and of a pre-war vintage. When I went to the Trucial Coast, it was with a Cirroflex (a fairly cheap American copy of the Rolleiflex) bought in Egypt in 1946. Later, I acquired a large antique Thornton Pickard quarter-plate reflex camera, beautifully made and with a superb Cooke lens in a large brass mount. It was a joy to play with but, as plates were hard to find, I obtained a large roll-film adaptor which was a disaster as it scratched tramlines on the whole length of the film. Had I kept that camera, it would today be a valuable collectors' item. Instead, I disposed of it to someone who, I was later told, preferred it for its size and potential use for gold smuggling!

On a later visit to Bahrain, I treated myself to a newly arrived, post-war Rolleiflex, a quality camera of which my Cirroflex was but a poor imitation. The Rolleiflex has been used by many of the masters of photography since it came into being in the early 1930s, its main photographic limitations being a relatively wide-angle, non-interchangeable lens with a maximum aperture of only f3.5 and, of course, no exposure aid. Even so, it was a splendid camera, but a somewhat heavy addition to the already-large bag of equipment which I constantly lugged around with me.

Although my preference was, and has remained, for monochrome work, I tried a few rolls of 120-size Ektachrome colour film which had just arrived on the market. With a speed rating of ASA 25, it was regarded as fast! I developed monochrome films myself, but sent my Ektachromes to Wallace Heaton in London for processing. The results when they finally arrived back, although good, did not win me over to colour photography, and I found the 6x6-cm transparencies (negative colour film had yet to be invented) rather frustrating, for I had neither the means of making prints from them, nor of projecting them, other than through my enlarger in my makeshift darkroom.

They were, however, sufficiently good to whet the appetite of the National Geographic Society when they approached me for an article for their famous magazine. Contrary to the trend at the time, the magazine was one of the early pioneers of 35-mm colour work, so I was advised to buy myself a Leica and shoot Kodachrome. At the first

opportunity, I made another shopping trip to Bahrain. I should explain that, at that time, Bahrain was a popular shopping centre used by expatriates from around the Gulf to obtain goods and luxuries which were not available in the places where they worked (or, indeed, in austere post-war Britain).

I was unable to find a Leica, which was just as well, as I was not keen on direct viewfinders and their limitations when using interchangeable lenses. Instead, I found an Exakta, the first single-lens reflex 35-mm camera, which had progressively developed through various models since the early 1930s. As a single-lens reflex devotee, it has been pleasing to me to see the extent to which it has become the camera of the present, particularly after the invention of built-in metering. Even so, I might have done better with the unrivalled Leica lenses.

I still have my Exakta and Rolleiflex, worn and with one or two dents, but working. They have served me well and I sometimes feel unfaithful for abandoning them, but it is difficult to ignore the luxury of a modern camera with automatic exposure controls.

Considering that they are more than 40 years old and have been stored in variable, adverse conditions, largely in hot climes, my Kodachromes have survived well, but the passage of time has not been so kind to my Ektachromes. This bears out a

This photograph of Ronald Codrai and his wife Pamela was appropriately taken against a backdrop of Dubai Creek – a place which features so strongly in this book – during a visit to the Emirate in 1988.

camera, it was later made available for still photography. With a film speed of only ASA 8, it was very limiting compared with monochrome film, although even that had a top speed at the time of only ASA 100. As a result, I continued to take photographs in both types. Another problem was in obtaining fresh films and materials, and I found that I was receiving chemicals in tins sometimes so rusty that a finger could be pushed through them, while others must have been stored very close to ships' boilers. Several times I developed monochrome film, only to find it completely fogged.

The situation gradually improved as the market settled down to post-war conditions, demand increased and there was greater turnover of supplies and availability of fresh stock. Later, Kodachrome did not present a problem in that regard as fresh consignments were sent to me from America, although it took quite a time for them to be processed and returned, and some were lost *en route*. At the time there was a great deal of difference between the quality of the processing in England, France and America. America led the way with France arguably second.

I developed all my monochrome films myself; water and temperature were the main difficulties. Well water had to be filtered, which was tedious, and it was very revealing to see what the filters held back. The films dried slowly when it was humid but, on occasions and without notice, an absolutely dry, hot wind would start to blow off the desert causing the films to dry almost instantly. They would curl into an arc and then whip straight with a loud crack, often leaving damaging watermarks, not to mention pinholes from sand stuck to the emulsion.

My first enlarger I made myself, eventually graduating to the comparative luxury of one that I purchased, albeit a fairly simple affair. Enlarging was great fun, and I enjoyed enormously seeing the results of my camera work and experimenting in the darkroom. I had to economise on my use of sweet water or else arrange for a steady stream of donkeys to carry water from the wells. As this was neither practical nor cheap, I mostly took my enlargements swimming with me in the sea, since salt water is very effective in removing the fixing agent from the paper, after which the salt was removed with a few rinses of sweet water. One of the drawbacks I discovered, however, was that some photographic paper sank and had to be retrieved

recent study on the durability of colour films, which reached much the same conclusion. Many other colour films have since appeared on the market but the difficulty is that the only true test of time is the passage of time itself. Then, if cherished pictures begin to fade, it's too late. You can never be certain, but it's sad to think that so many of today's photographs may not survive in the same way as some of the monochrome treasures of the last century, particularly those taken on negative colour film and processed in doubtful conditions.

Kodachrome was first produced as a cine film but, with the growing popularity of the 35-mm

by diving to the bottom. I therefore kept a somewhat bizarre list showing which photographic paper sank and which floated in the sea – information not provided by the manufacturers!

Photography is a great hobby. Many years ago I met a missionary who shared my interest in it. He and his wife invited me to their Spartan house in the Lebanese hills where I was proudly shown his tiny, improvised darkroom. He had made his enlarger and his darkroom lights himself, and the developing dishes were from the kitchen. On a small, angled and recessed wooden block he carefully placed his pocket watch which, fortunately, had a large second-hand. What he

lacked in equipment he made up for with skill and enthusiasm. He and his wife lived rather austerely and, as he broke the seal on a small packet of enlarging paper, he said that he felt guilty at his extravagance. Then, he held his fingertips together and uttered, "For this, my hobby, may the Lord make me truly grateful."

Fifty years later, I can but add "Amen."

**ABOVE: Ronald Codrai with a fine barracuda – you can read more about his adventures with this fish on page 31.
LEFT: Ronald Codrai photographed prior to setting out on a journey to Oman in April 1948.**

National Bank of Dubai

The National Bank of Dubai

The National Bank of Dubai, the first local bank in the UAE, has strong historical links with the sea and the seafarers of the Emirates. These include the position of its striking new head office building, overlooking the Creek and the Gulf beyond; the actual shape of the building, reminiscent of a sail; the bank's links with Sultan Al-Owais, one of its founders and its first Chairman; and, more recently, a purpose-built museum that houses the priceless collection of pearls Sultan Al-Owais donated to the people of the UAE under the custodianship of the bank.

The bank was established, under a Charter granted by HH the late Sheikh Rashid bin Saeed Al Maktoum, Ruler of Dubai, by a group of prominent Dubai merchants and commenced operations in Dubai on May 9, 1963.

From the beginning, all normal commercial banking services were provided and the bank was able to show a modest profit in its first report. It received good support from the government and the business community.

In June 1966, the Indian Rupee, which was then the currency in use in the Gulf, was sharply devalued. As a result of dissatisfaction with this decision, Rupees were withdrawn from circulation in Dubai and temporarily replaced by Saudi Riyals until the Qatar/Dubai Riyal was introduced. The National Bank of Dubai was officially appointed agent for the Qatar/Dubai Currency Board.

In 1973 the UAE Currency Board was established and the Dirham adopted as local currency. The National Bank of Dubai was appointed the Currency Board's agent for the six Northern Emirates.

To cater for its expanding business, the bank's head office moved to large new premises in Baniyas Road in March 1970. The opening ceremony was performed by HH Sheikh Rashid bin Saeed Al Maktoum, Ruler of Dubai, and the event was commemorated with a special stamp issue.

In 1970, shipments of crude oil commenced from Dubai and the next decade witnessed a tremendous upsurge in business and development activity. The bank was well established by this time and was able to participate in and support the vastly increased demands for commercial, housing and project finance as well as being closely involved in many development projects

successfully executed by the Dubai Government.

To sustain this growth, the bank's own funds were progressively increased from AED 35 million in 1973 to AED 3,445 million by 1990. Although the number of banks operating in the country had risen to 47 by the latter date, the National Bank of Dubai retained its pre-eminent position. Meanwhile, deposits broke through the AED one billion barrier in 1976 and the AED10 billion mark in 1984.

In 1980, the Central Bank Act was introduced in order to organise and promote the banking industry – an industry that had proliferated in a very short period. Because of its consistent policy of conservative banking, the National Bank of Dubai was readily able to comply with the new directives and norms.

In 1981, in pursuance of the policy of encouraging local participation in banks, the Central Bank advised all National banks that at least 80 per cent of their share-holding should be with UAE nationals. Accordingly, the National Bank of Dubai arranged a repurchase of foreign shareholders' interest and, since 1982, more than 82 per cent of its shares have been locally owned.

A branch was established in Sloane Street, London, in 1986 and another four years later in Jersey, giving the bank the distinction of being the first Arab bank to be granted a licence by the Channel Islands authorities.

The bank celebrated its 25th anniversary in 1988 – an event that was commemorated by a special stamp issue. By then 96 per cent of the shares were locally held. Under the able guidance of the bank's directors, most of whom had been on the Board since its inception, the bank had consistently maintained a record of high profitability and growth during its first 25 years. Profits grew from Rupees 111,000 in 1964 to AED 396 million in 1988, and the total assets from Rupees 39 million to AED 22 billion. The bank ranked at 213 out of the top 500 banks of the world – the highest ranking for any UAE bank. It also enjoyed the highest AA+ rating of any bank in the Gulf.

Profits continued to improve during the next two years, peaking at AED 466 million in 1990 with total assets standing at AED 24 billion. However, there was to be an economic slowdown in the 1990s and the sluggish conditions were to present the UAE banking industry with difficult challenges. Nevertheless, the bank's conservative policies, that had sustained its growth over many years, enabled it to continue its support for major projects of the Dubai Government.

Economic conditions notwithstanding, a number of new branches were opened between 1994 and 1999. Another notable landmark was the inauguration, in February 1998, of the new Headquarters building by HH Sheikh Hamdan bin Rashid Al Maktoum.

The year 1999 was a busy one for the bank and a number of key areas to meet the challenges of the new millennium were identified by the directors. The development of National employees was a high priority.

In January 2000, the death of Sultan Ali Al-Owais, who had been Chairman of the bank since its formation, came as a great shock to his colleagues. His wise counsel had played a key role in guiding the policies of the bank and his passing away was an irreparable loss to the bank.

During 2000 the bank reorganised its management and operating processes after completing a strategic review of its business. Other highlights of the year included *The Banker* magazine voting the National Bank of Dubai first among UAE banks in terms of capital adequacy, winning the Emiratisation Award for the second successive year, the opening of more branches, the appointment of HE Dr Khalifa Mohamed Sulaiman as Chairman and the appointment of the first female UAE National Manager at a new branch in Al Mizhar.

Although 2001 will be remembered for the dreadful events in New York on September 11 and the subsequent decline in the world economy, the UAE banking sector remained strong. In Dubai the Anti Money Laundering Law was enacted, the Dubai International Financial Centre was announced, and the city was designated to host the prestigious IMF-World Bank 2003 meetings, with the National Bank of Dubai playing an important role in promoting this prestigious event.

Total assets grew during 2001 by 16 per cent to AED 32 billion and the bank's net profit increased to AED 452 million. In 2002 the bank was voted Best Bank in the UAE by *The Banker*.

The bank today

Prudent policies, coupled with major investment in technology and professional management, have made the National Bank of Dubai one of the soundest and most successful financial institutions in the Middle East. From its imposing new Headquarters it operates 33 branches and pay offices in the UAE plus a fully automated branch in Grand Cineplex and one retail branch in London.

One sign of the bank's success is its consistent profitability. It has earned top ratings from business publications and is described as among the best capitalised banks in the Gulf. A policy of conservatism has meant significant provision of value for shareholders in the form of bonus shares in addition to high dividends.

The bank has a long history of banking excellence. Its retail service philosophy combines the Arab tradition of hospitality and care with the efficiency and precision of modern technology. The bank's mission is to establish itself as the preferred neighbourhood or 'high street' bank, providing easily accessible and dependable banking support to people across the Emirates.

Complementing its branch network throughout the Emirates are its off-site ATMs. The bank pioneered the first stand-alone ATM in the UAE in 1986 and today customers can withdraw cash and pay utility bills through a network of more than 92 ATMs, as well as utilise the point-of-sale terminals installed at a large number of hotels and stores.

The National Bank of Dubai has an ongoing commitment to provide training and development opportunities, to enable UAE nationals to build banking careers and help the development of the UAE.

The treasures of Sultan Al-Owais

O sea! O sea!
This is the pearl of the land
Have you in the cradles of your shells
a pearl to match?

Sultan Al-Owais was one of Dubai's most important pearl merchants, poets and philanthropists. Born in 1925 to a cultured, well-to-do family, he grew up in the village of Al Hira where regular visits to his father's library nurtured his love for poetry. His father, Ali Al-Owais, was a pearl merchant, and as a young man Sultan would accompany him on business trips. Year after year, he developed business skills that would eventually lead him to become one of the most successful businessmen of his time.

He travelled to India to continue his pearl trading in 1948 but the decline of the pearl industry began soon after and he returned to Dubai to explore further ventures in trade, land brokerage and banking. In 1963 he was appointed Chairman of the National Bank of Dubai – a position he held until his death on January 4, 2000.

Sultan Al-Owais began collecting pearls in the early 70s. Thirty years later he had assembled one of the largest pearl collections in the world, constituting a large number of 'Oriental' (salt-water) pearls. Some of the finest pearls of the Gulf are part of this collection. Exquisite pieces of perfectly round unblemished silver-white pearls of metallic lustre crown the finest lots, while a variety of cream, gold, silver, rose and grey pearls of shapes varying from baroque to drop form the rest.

He donated his collection to the people of the UAE under the custodianship of the National Bank of Dubai and it is now housed in a purpose-built museum in the bank's headquarters building.

As one of the most prominent philanthropists in the history of the UAE, Sultan Al-Owais donated hundreds of millions of Dirhams throughout his life, for the construction of hospitals, mosques, dams and schools in the UAE and other Arab countries. He also established an annual prize for scientific achievement for UAE citizens and the prestigious prize for culture that carries his name (it is interesting to note that, in 1993, Ronald Codrai was the first non-Arab to win this award).

Though considered to be one of the region's most esteemed poets, he renounced fame and recognition. His poetry was driven by an internal need, with no desire for showcasing his achievements, so much so that if his work had not been collected and published by his friends it never would have reached us and, in the process, a true 'treasure' would have remained hidden forever.

Acknowledgements

It is always a difficult task trying to complete an unfinished work left by someone else, particular so in the case of this book where Ronald, my father, had such a clear idea as to how he wanted the finished product to look. Trying to marry this objective to those of the publisher was, therefore, never going to be an easy task. Consequently, once again, the Codrai family is eternally grateful to Ian Fairservice for his helpfulness, support, willingness and loyalty in agreeing to publish this book. Without him, Ronald's wishes might well have proved unachievable and this splendid book would not have seen the light of day.

As always, it is the Motivate Publishing team that has helped to shape the book and, in addition to Ian Fairservice, the family is particularly indebted to David Steele, Zelda Pinto and Johnson Machado – as well as Alison Ashbee and Jackie Nel – who have all done an admirable job of editing and laying out the book and tying together all the loose ends.

The family is also particularly grateful to the National Bank of Dubai for agreeing to sponsor the book in conjunction with the opening of the Pearl Museum at its Headquarters. It is particularly fitting that it should undertake the sponsorship as Sultan Al-Owais, the bank's founder (in whose honour the Pearl Museum was founded) was, amongst other things, a pearl merchant in the era to which this book relates. Our thanks go to the bank for its help in preserving this colourful and historically important slice of the United Emirates' past.

Justin Codrai

بنك دبي الوطني

National Bank of Dubai

Published with the encouragement and support of the National Bank of Dubai.